"Bittersweet"

Cheddleton Memories

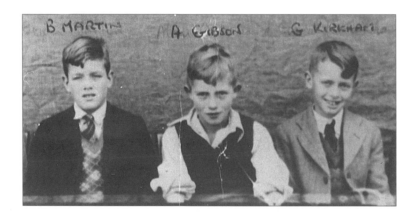

by

ALAN GIBSON

CHURNET VALLEY BOOKS
1 King Street, Leek, Staffordshire. 01538 399033
email: picture.book@virgin.net web: freespace.virgin.net/c.hinton/
Printed in Malta by Interprint Limited
© Alan Gibson and Churnet Valley Books 2000
ISBN 1 897949 69 3

Dedication
To the class of '49

Acknowledgements

Thank you to all my friends and acquaintances who have kindly provided the photographs contained within this book and to whom I hope I have correctly credited each of them. May I also thank: Rev. Chris Brown and Sue Hall for their continuous support, Mrs S. Grace (née Hanrahan), former directors of Brittains Ltd, Mrs W McCarron, Mrs J. Jones, and all who have contributed in so many ways. And most importantly my wife Vera.

Photograph acknowledgements
E. Alcock, R. Alcock, R. Bold, Mrs M. Berresford, Roger Coghill, A. Corden, Max Chadwick, Geoffrey Fisher, Mrs A. Hedley, Barbara Hobson, Mrs P. Harris, Basil Jeuda, R.N. Ogden, Mrs M. Pegg, Ray Poole, Mrs R. Salmon, St Edwards Hospital, York Railway Museum

Author's note
Chapter Seven: The information was derived from public records, newspapers and directors of Brittain's Paper Mills, including a full report of the events recorded by a director of the company as and when they occurred. Other information supports this record of events but was considered too sensitive to print. All information was received in confidence.

Contents

The March of Time

When the tint of the rose has fled from the glass
And it's reality that dwells in the eye
You have learned the lesson from life's master class
It is age you cannot defy

When the fox trots quickly away from the floor
And the song of the dance lies unsung
When the triumphs of life you can count by the score
But victory remains with the young

When the slow march of time is always too fast
And you are going along at a pace
There's still time to dwell on times that are past
Whilst others continue the race

But don't dwell too long on what might have been
It's far better to look straight ahead
There's much to be done and much to be seen
And it is better to lead than be led

For sweet voices unheard and heroes unsung
Still litter the pathway of life
And not always do they belong to the young
But those who have shared the same strife

For the pleasures of life are still to be gained
If we make of it all what we can
And sway to the tune of life's sweet refrain
.......That's the thoughts of a Cheddleton man

Three official images
produced during the
First World War.

Chapter One
Nerves of Steel

Sarajevo - Bosnia. June 1914

Gavrilo Princip listened intently to the words of his mentor, Dragutin Dimitrijevic, or Apis as he was known to members of the notorious Black Hand Society. The factions within Bosnia-Herzegovina had long been at odds with their Austro-Hungarian masters and ethnic emotions, constantly stirred by extremists, did nothing to ease matters. For Gavrilo and his fellow conspirators the deadly instructions now being issued were stark and final. The Archduke Franz Ferdinand, heir to the Austro-Hungarian throne, and his wife, were to be assassinated. The weapons with which the conspirators were armed were supplied by the Society and, as the meeting broke up, Gavrilo and his friends quietly concealed the firearms and faded away.

June 28th 1914

A bright sunny day. The Archduke and his wife walked towards the municipal buildings in Sarajevo. Around them strode the usual accompaniment of uniformed guards and dignitaries. The mixed and restive crowd gave the royal couple a muted reception; the jostling amongst them was no more than was expected. Then a sudden eruption within a few metres of the Archduke found him staring at a wild eyed Gavrilo and his cohort. Taken completely by surprise the Archduke and his retinue looked on in horror as Gavrilo Princip raised his arms and fired several shots at close range. Even as the guards leapt upon the assassin, the Archduke and his wife were falling to the ground.

As the shock waves reverberated around the world, Austria-Hungary determined to take the strongest action against Serbia. There was no evidence to show that the Serbian government was involved in the murders. If anything they were embarrassed about the whole affair. They were aware, of course, of the Black Hand Society, but the assassination had taken them equally and completely by surprise.

The capture of the assasins in Sarajevo, Bosnia - the photograph that flashed around the World in 1914.
The incident led to the First World War.

July 23rd 1914

The Austro-Hungarian government issued an ultimatum to Serbia that was most humiliating. The Serbs, still shocked and uncertain, accepted all the conditions except one, namely that Austro-Hungarian soldiers should enter Serbia and eliminate the remaining Sarajevo conspirators. In response to this refusal the Austro-Hungarian government declared war on Serbia on the 28th of July.

Witnessing these events from across the border, the Germans felt the Gods were smiling on them. Russia, which was quickly growing into a dominant power, had threatened Germany's European superiority. As long ago as 1905 and 1906, the German Chief of Staff, Alfred von Schlieffer, had wanted to invade Russia and quell what he saw as a growing menace.

Germany's chance arrived on the back of Austria and Serbia's misfortunes and was seized upon. On the 30th of July Russia mobilised its forces in support of Serbia, to discourage further aggression by Austria-Hungary. Germany, ostensibly in support of Austria, declared war on Russia. On the 1st and the 3rd of August they also declared war on France, for reasons that were totally unclear, although the two countries had been at each other's throats for a long time. Germany demanded free access through Belgium which was promptly refused by Belgium's neutral government.

August 4th 1914

Britain looked on in alarm. She was a close ally of Belgium, and had already entered into a pact which meant that Britain would defend Belgium's neutrality in the event of war. So Britain declared war on Germany and became involved in a brutal and bloody conflict that would be four years of hell on the continent of Europe and would cost millions of lives.

As news of the war spread throughout the country, the British propaganda machine also gathered momentum. Newspaper articles denouncing the Germans and extolling the virtues of Britain and her empire promoted a feeling of pride and invincibility. Young men from every walk of life volunteered in their thousands, as Britain's army, untrained and unsung, prepared to fight for freedom and democracy. Those who hesitated were vilified and treated with contempt. Willing or unwilling, everyone found themselves preparing for war.

Aston Manor, a small suburb on the outskirts of Birmingham was a real hive of activity. The area, a mixture of park land and houses, was finally giving way to the endless pressure of Birmingham's expansion and in the middle of this Edwardian growth and prosperity the Jones family had thrived. Their small family firm of jobbing builders had quickly adapted to the demand for houses and factories. The family's future was looking very rosy indeed and they were totally unprepared for the sudden announcement by their youngest son Jack that he had volunteered to join the Rifle Brigade.

His father kindly explained to Jack that he was too young to join the army. *"Sorry Dad,"* he replied, *"I told them I was eighteen and I have been accepted."* In a matter of days Jack had received official acceptance and instructions of where to report for training.

As the weeks flew by Jack and his fellow volunteers became familiar with the disciplines of army life. *'Obey! Obey! Obey! Do not question orders, do not hesitate, and remember at all times that your Officers are equipped mentally and physically to cope with the demands of war.'* Confidence could not have been higher amongst the new troops. It was generally thought that it would all be over by Christmas. This led to an eagerness to complete training and quickly join those in Belgium and France who were already *'teaching the Hun a lesson.'*

Early in November the fresh recruits, their training completed, left their barracks at Stratford and were taken by train to Portsmouth where troop ships awaited their arrival. In the early hours of the following morning the ships departed and by day-break were in sight of the Belgian coast. A rapid disembarkement followed, and the troops were transported in convoys of lorries and trains to various destinations to join their regiments. Jack, still wet behind the ears, found himself travelling towards the town of Ypres. Jack's regiment was camped a few miles from the town and were within an hour of major action.

The scene at the camp brought the first realities of war home. Soldiers, who only weeks or days ago had arrived at the camp, were returning from the front line. Ambulances, field hospitals, the wounded and the dying gave Jack his first experience of what life, or rather death, was all about. For the first time he regretted his decision to volunteer as with a heavy heart he joined his comrades and silently settled in. He quickly struck up a friendship with Michael Pearson, a private from Stoke-on-Trent, and like Jack, an eager volunteer. Keeping a fatherly eye on all of them was Sergeant Chapman, a veteran of thirty, who presence was made felt before they even thought of commiting a misdemeanour!

Chapman became the bane of their young lives as he set out to instil even greater discipline. When he said jump, they jumped. They had been at the camp only a couple of weeks when they received orders to prepare for battle and the following day, a grey, damp morning, a fleet of lorries dropped several hundred novices a miles or so behind the wet, muddy trenches that were to become their homes for the next few months. All thoughts of being home by Christmas soon disappeared. To their dismay, Jack and Michael discovered that Sergeant Chapman, instead of being left at base camp, was to be with them permanently.

Life in the trenches held none of the romance of the story books, and bore even less resemblance to the military manuals their training had been based upon. During the December of 1914 the British troops tried in vain to gain ground against German troops who seemed better trained and better equipped. Time and time again British officers led waves of men out of the trenches to attack the German positions. Heavy artillery fire, intended to cover the advance, had little effect on the enemy. Shells either fell short of the target or, more often than not, were landing hundreds of yards behind.

The Germans, having assessed the situation more accurately, simply met the British advances with a barrage of rifle and machine gun fire. The results were devastating. British troops died in their thousands without gaining the advantage. As Jack, Michael, Chapman and the other survivors dragged themselves back to the relative safety of their trenches, the German heavy artillery took over. Although not much more accurate than the British, the constant bombardment kept them constantly occupied whilst giving the German troops time to make their own attacks.

In those opening months only sheer guts and determination saved the British. Inept leadership bordering on stupidity sent more and more men to an inglorious and muddy death. The British were unable to inflict more than a meagre list of casualties. The pattern of war was only to change as Britain came to terms with its own shortcomings and, slowly but surely, set about the task of improving its leadership, its tactics and its professionalism.

As 1914 turned to 1915 and then to 1916, young men from all over the world died in the pursuit of freedom. Survivors, mentally scarred or wounded, fought on as the tide slowly turned. Shell-shocked and weary the young became familiar with death, mutilation and destruction. One particular horrific event was to remain with Jack for the rest of his life. In the late afternoon of an autumn day an assault on the German lines was planned. The men from Jack's trench rose en masse and raced forward. Lately they had been gaining a little ground, small important victories giving a renewed confidence to those becoming cynical. They were met with the usual hail of bullets and shells.

Jack and Michael, together as always, cursed the unexpected accuracy and threw themselves to the ground. Jack wiped away the mud and rain from his face only to discover that he was spattered with blood. He turned to his mate; *"Hell fire, Mike, that was too bloody close,"* and then stopped. All that remained of Michael Pearson were a few fragments of uniform and bits of blood and gore. The shell that hit Michael a split second before he dived to the ground exploded on impact and simply blew him to pieces. Nothing remained. No body, no victory, no glorious return. Nothing to bury; nothing to praise.

Jack lay among the debris of battle too shocked to move. He lost recollection of time or events until a hand grabbed him roughly by the collar. Sergeant Chapman, in no mood for gentle persuasion, yanked him to his feet *"Run, for Christ's sake,"* and with Chapman still holding him they raced for the trenches where he was bundled to safety.

The loss of his friend in such an appalling way affected Jack deeply. That night in the privacy of darkness he sat in a damp corner of the trench and wept the tears of war, the tears that flow freely when the truth is seen. A few yards away the watchful Chapman guarded the moment and ensured no intrusion as Jack unburdened his soul.

The following morning as the trench stirred Chapman assumed his usual and expected role, and the men prepared, once again, to advance. For Jack and a few of the wounded a return to base had been arranged and at first light he joined with men from the Ambulance Brigade and was returned to relative safety. The peace of the base camp and the euphoria that follows the relief of battle swept over the men. Men recovered as days turned into weeks. Refreshed, clean, but far from ready to return to the affray Jack counted the days off, until all too soon, they were taken back to their units. He was greeted by Sergeant Wilson who, tarred with the same brush as all sergeants, brusquely established his authority.

As he stood once again in the trenches Jack looked around for a familiar face. Even during his short absence new recruits had replaced old hands. Recognising one or two he received a nod or a wave. Of Sergeant Chapman he could see no sign and at the first opportunity he approached Sergeant Wilson to enquire *"Where's Sergeant Chapman these days?"* Wilson hesitated then said, *"How well did you know him?"* *"Pretty well really, he was with us from the beginning,"* replied Jack. Wilson hesitated again *"Well he won't be with you any more; you've got me now. Sergeant Chapman was killed in action a few days ago. He stopped to help one of his men and got caught in rifle fire."*

Jack, silenced once more, looked again at the new faces and tried to remember the names of all those who had gone. Faces and names remained. Good ones, bad ones. Quips and anecdotes sprung to mind, bringing a smile to mask the pain, as once again he prepared himself for the next day. Survival became the essential need, as the tide of battle turned in favour of the British. Survive at all costs, do not die now.

As 1917 approached the veterans took more and more ground. As is often the case, death and destruction are countered with emotion and joy. The most poignant of all occurred on Christmas Eve. In the silence of that night men of both sides, savouring the peace, gazed across the pitted battle fields. Candles were being lit along a never ending line and a sense of peace and tranquillity swept over everyone. The murmuring of the men subsided until there was absolute silence. Quiet tears and thoughts of home lengthened the silence until it was suddenly broken by the sweet tenor voice of a German soldier. As he sang, the words were picked up by a British voice and then by more men on both sides.

Stille Nacht, heilige nacht,   *All is dark, save the light,*
Nor das traute, hochleilige paar   *Oer the Babe who in silent sleep*
Schlaeft in himmlische Ruh   *Rests in heavenly peace*
                                         Rests in heavenly peace

For a few moments the world was at peace.

Holy night, Silent night
All is calm, all is bright
Around yon virgin mother, and child
Holy infant so tender and mild
Sleep in heavenly peace
Sleep in heavenly peace.

Stille nacht, heilige nacht,
Gottes sohn, oh wie lacht
Leib aus deinem goettichen mund
Da und schlaegt die rettende stund
Christ in deiner geburt
Christ in deiner geburt.

The start of 1918 saw the beginning of the end of the Great War. Allied resilience and determination had broken the German spirit. Belgium was re-occupied. Throughout the spring and summer the German retreat became a flood. Old soldiers, young soldiers, officers and men allowed themselves at last to believe the end was in sight.

As the summer turned to autumn, hopes and rumours became fact. The mighty German war machine had finally been broken. At 11.00am, on the 11th of November 1918, Germany signed the surrender. Millions lay dead on the battle fields of France and Belgium, and in Russia and Austria. Those that returned to their native lands were scarred and worn out by the bloodiest conflict of man upon man in history. Democracy and right had triumphed at an incalculable cost - and thoughts of returning to a 'land fit for heroes' soon disappeared as austerity gripped a nation recovering from the costs of war.

After Jack's return to Aston Manor he was anxious to re-establish himself as a member of the family and to pick up the threads of his career. The War had put paid to his apprenticeship but he eagerly anticipated a period of learning and a welcome back to the family business. He was to be bitterly disappointed. During his absence one of his in-laws had been quick to establish himself and in a very short time had not only managed to replace Jack, but had become indispensable. There was simply no room, with the economic situation as it was. He was out of favour and out of a job. The only light on the horizon was Tilly Coe.

Tilly had lived all her life in Leek in Staffordshire and as the War progressed she, along with many others, was seconded to help the War effort. She had been transferred to a munitions factory in Birmingham and placed in the care of the Jones family for board and lodgings. To the family's disgust and to Tilly's delight, the pair fell in love. For the family it turned into an ideal opportunity to resolve the problem of Jack. Tilly, homesick and fed up, was determined to return to Leek and to the silk mills she knew - and the Jones family were only too pleased to help.

Within a few months the pair were married and set for a life that was very familiar to Tilly, but alien to Jack. Despite the recession Jack managed to find employment in Cheddleton, a village about three miles away from Leek, where a huge asylum was still being built. Jack was to remain in the employ of the maintenance department of this mental hospital for the rest of his working life.

Over the years five children were born to the Jones's and it became Jack's habit to relate tales of the Great War to his children. As time went on the facts became more hazy and the deeds of valour increased - and it became a well-known fact among the children that their father had "nerves of steel". It all became too much for one child, Jack Junior, whose imagination ran away with him. He decided to test his Dad's nerves. One very cold night, the moment of reckoning arrived. Young Jack went to bed at about 9.30 but instead of going to his own bed he crept into his parents' room and lay silently under the bed. About an hour and a half later Jack and Tilly came to bed and settled down for the night. Still young Jack lay there. Finally in the dead of night, absolutely frozen, he slid from beneath the bed. Very gently he lifted the eiderdown, the blanket and the sheet and, as Jack's feet were exposed, young Jack grasped them with both hands.

Now it has to be said that Jack senior did not believe in levitation, but his son swears to this day that his father rose at least a foot off the bed and shrieked, *"Oh my God, the buggers have got me."* What happened to Jack junior is not recorded but the nerves of steel reputation of his father took a bit of a battering!

As for Jack and Tilly's other children, none remained in Cheddleton or Leek. However, one grandchild manage to remain in Cheddleton long enough to attend the village school and eventually to marry the writer of this story. Vera Adams was to become my wife and for a while she followed the footsteps of her grandfather as a nurse at St. Edward's Hospital.

The hospital where Jack Jones Senior spent the rest of his working life was totally different to the relaxed attitude of today's hospitals and St. Edward's was virtually self sufficient with farms and gardens providing all basic foods, a boiler house and turbine room providing heat and electricity and a host of tradesmen with every form of skill imaginable.

Discipline within the wards was harsh in the extreme and respect was demanded almost to the touching of the forelock. If the medical orderlies, doctors, matrons and sisters were gods on the wards, the foremen, managers and supervisors acted like gods elsewhere. The discipline was still much in evidence as I was growing up. By the time I was old enough to wander around the village the hospital or asylum as we called it was part of my domain. I knew some of the boys who lived along Wall Lane Terrace. Doug Grub, Jimmy Black, Roger Orme and Ian Blenkinsop all had parents employed by the hospital.

Paul Rose was part of a large family supported by the efforts of a hard working mother. They scraped along on a wing and a prayer and were just about as poverty stricken as we were. When Paul was available we wandered the grounds in a sort of semi-official capacity.

Wall Lane Terrace.

St Edward's Hospital.

St Edward's Hospital being built in 1897.

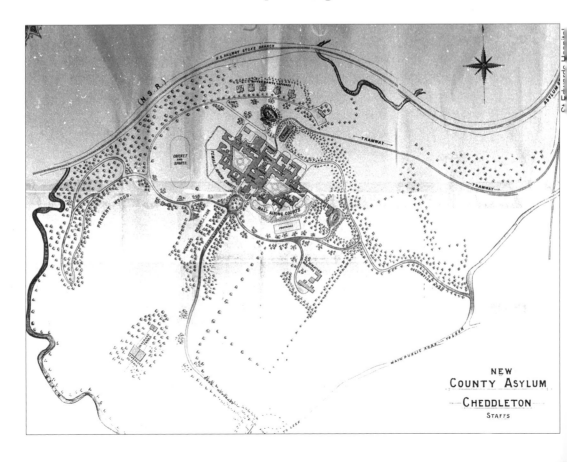

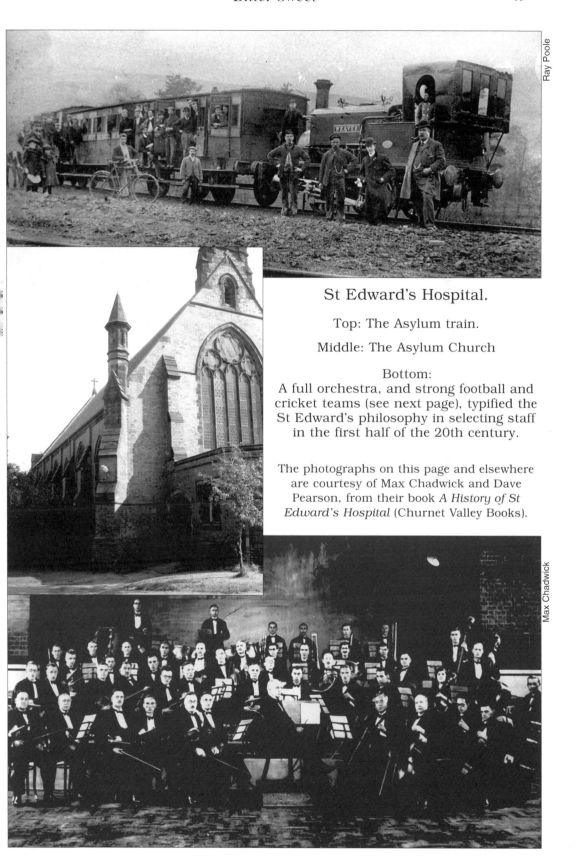

Ray Poole

Max Chadwick

St Edward's Hospital.

Top: The Asylum train.

Middle: The Asylum Church

Bottom:
A full orchestra, and strong football and cricket teams (see next page), typified the St Edward's philosophy in selecting staff in the first half of the 20th century.

The photographs on this page and elsewhere are courtesy of Max Chadwick and Dave Pearson, from their book *A History of St Edward's Hospital* (Churnet Valley Books).

A football team at St Edward's Hospital about 1920.

St Edward's Hospital, matron and sisters, between the Wars.

Employee's children were tolerated and had the freedom of the hospital. When Paul was not available I managed to seek out every nook and cranny on my own. I was as familiar with the hospital as any employee.

Many of the patients were employed by the various trade departments but even the most humble labourer had two or three men at his disposal. For the most part, the patients were treated well enough but a lack of tolerance and verbal and physical abuse were not uncommon.

Over the years a hierarchy had developed that ran from top to bottom. People who would have made little impression elsewhere would strive for promotion and upon gaining a supervisory position became members of a management structure that gave them a sense of power far in excess of their actual position. The storeman was feared, the trade foreman respected and obeyed, and the works engineer who had little enough to do nevertheless merited a well qualified assistant. When the lowest of the low got fed up of being at everyone's beck and call they had the dubious distinction of giving orders to the patients. The patients, bless them, were usually too far gone to give a damn about anything and usually chose to ignore what did not suit them.

The army of patients and staff was sufficient to keep the hospital grounds in immaculate condition. The football and cricket pitches were maintained to a professional standard and the gardens grew enough crops to not only supplement the hospital kitchens but to feed the families of employees who managed to augment their incomes by taking home a bag of vegetables or fruit. I do not suppose it will ever be admitted but pilfering was rife. Sheets and blankets would disappear from the wards and no doubt the shoemaker and the plumber had a full order book of foreigners. It was common knowledge that the hospital farm housed cattle for local farmers who gained a good income when the fatted calf was sold at Leek market.

On the recreational side the hospital tended to look after its staff better than its patients. The arguement was that the stress of looking after the mentally ill was such that nurses were employed only if their outside interests were sufficient enough to relieve the pressure. Very often people were selected more because of their extra-mural activities than their nursing ability. Ex-professional musicians, footballers and cricketers proliferated. As a result St. Edward's had a fine orchestra and a sporting reputation to be proud of. Little wonder each section basked in its own glory at the top of its particular tree. With facilities second to none and professional players in plenty the forties and fifties was a golden era for St. Edward's.

The main relief for patients came in the form of bus trips, hospital dances and the weekly film show. The film show was held in the main hall and was looked forward to as much by me and my friends as by the patients. Quite how we managed to sneak into the hall I don't know. I can only conclude that my demeanour and mental capacity allowed me to mix freely with my peers! What I remember clearly is not so much the films as the distractions. Some of the patients had a very short concentration span and would move around or fall out with each other. Most distracting was the actions of the artistic. Just as Tarzan was about to wrestle a crocodile to its death a shadow would appear on the screen. A bored patient, raising his arms into the light of the projecting beam would try to make a shape with his hands and a profile of a duck would drift across the screen. The bedlam that followed was akin to the Palace at Leek when we went to see the cowboy film on a Saturday afternoon.

Some of the more stable patients were allowed to work in the village and would often be seen on the local farms. In truth not all were insane. The aftermath of Victorian rectitude remained for many years. Old ladies, long since institutionalised, had been placed in care for the crime of having a child out of wedlock or being orphaned or difficult. Whether or not mental illness is contagious is not a subject for debate but I can recall doctors and workmen who showed all the signs of paranoia and habitual and obsessional procedures after spending a lifetime a St. Edward's.

Among the best known patients in the village was a very slim inoffensive man called Henry. He looked for all the world like Stan Laurel of Laurel and Hardy fame. Henry was the most gentle, friendly person and he spent most of his time outside the hospital living with the Turners of Highfields. They obviously cared a great deal for him and I am sure their kindness helped Henry to survive the harsh regime of the patient hierarchy.

Perhaps my closest link with the patients came just after I was married. For a period of one year I took leave of my senses and accepted a job as a maintenance fitter in the hospital engineering department. The ease of the job was matched only by the low level of pay. One of my duties was to repair the presses in the laundry. These machines were controlled by a series of valves and compressed air and I would spend most of my time adjusting the valves or repairing pipework. When the repairs were complete the machines had to be tested. Having a man in the laundry always created a stir among the female patients, many of whom were sexually frustrated. On this particular occasion a patient by the name of Grace was working on the press I was testing. Grace was about fifteen stone with all the subtlety of a Sumo wrestler. As I walked towards the controls I noticed her walking towards me with a smile on her face. Before I could move she grabbed me and pulled me to her. "Come here little man" she said as she engulfed me in her arms and buried my head in her ample bosom.

What she had in mind for me I dread to think. I only know I was totally powerless. Not only did Grace look like a Sumo wrestler, she was as strong as one. There was no escape. It was only the prompt action of the supervisory staff that saved me. I was prised out of Grace's arms amidst much protestation from Grace and great hilarity from the supervisors. I got no sympathy from my workmates either. They had deliberately not told me about Grace and I was just the latest to experience her charms.

Grace was not my only problem. Far more serious was my financial plight. I simply could not afford to work at St. Edward's any longer.

On the other hand my wife discovered that St. Edward's offered her the best chance to earn some extra money as we saved towards a deposit for our first house. Vera's story of hospital life is far more pertinent than my own and can be found in chapter seven.

B. Hobson

100 years ago Cheddleton was a hive of industry - Brittains, the station, the canal basin, the flint mill, the Hospital, farming, coalmining and a brickworks.

Above: The official 'cutting of the first sod' at Coalpitford coal mine (1904 postcard)
Below: Wall Grange brickworks.

B. Hobson

The Golden Lion (now The Linden Tree) Ipstones.

Ipstones main road at the beginning of the 20th Century.

Chapter Two
The Way it Was

Are all families as mixed up as ours? When I examine the garbled history of Granny Johnson and consult the fading memory of ageing relatives I wonder if what I hear can be true.

Emily Barker was the only girl in a family of eight children. Born in Ipstones in about 1855 she had the privilege of what we would now call a middle class upbringing. Her father, my great, great-grandfather, obviously salvaged some money from his early profession as a lawyer. That was before he managed to bring disgrace to the family with his habitual drinking.

He arrived in Ipstones in the 1840s and took up residence in a substantial property from where he bred golden retrievers. He appears to have been quite successful as a dog breeder gaining a nation-wide reputation with sales as far away as the Scottish Highlands. The peak of his financial achievements was probably when a dog sold to a Scottish landowner decided it was not happy and, after months of wandering, arrived back at Ipstones.

Despite his success as a dog breeder the demon drink was in control and he did what any sensible addict would do. He took over the local pub! He remained as landlord of The Golden Lion for 38 years, until his demise, when he was no doubt given a boozer's farewell.

Emily's life of privilege continued at The Golden Lion and, after completing her education, her skills as a seamstress were put to good use. While her father ran the pub, Emily and her mother produced dresses for the people of Leek and many other villages in the area. The skill of dressmaking was common enough at the time but the dresses produced at The Golden Lion were in great demand. The summer months were particularly busy when they were besieged with orders to make dresses for May Queens, Carnival Queens and Maypole dancers plus, on one occasion, 20 dresses for the Club Day parade in Leek.

Most of the children were now reaching maturity and earning their living in a variety of professions. Knightley - yes that really was his name - after working as an insurance agent, emigrated to America and was shortly followed by Rowland, the brains of the family. Rowland was a writer, composer and organist. Quite where he acquired such abilities is beyond our comprehension for his musical talents seemed to by-pass the rest of us.

Emily was growing up, and with striking good looks and easy charm she was a popular figure in the village. A little too popular from all accounts! Her father, who still kept in touch with his legal associates, was visited from time to time by young solicitors and the like. Emily fell in love with one of these young men and embarked on an affair that was to become the talk of the village. The Victorian age had more than its fair share of hypocrisy and becoming pregnant outside wedlock was beyond the pale. Not only was Emily pregnant, she was abandoned by her lover who had fled the scene. Her desperate efforts to abort the pregnancy failed when a herbal medical potion, known as Penny Royal, had no effect.

With a heavy heart she broke the news to her father. His reaction was predictable and furious. Despite Emily's condition, which she had managed to hide for almost four months, she was bundled into a carriage and four, and, with two postillions hanging on for dear life, they drove poste-haste to apprehend the missing lover. Her father, six foot two and weighing sixteen stone, carried a horse whip which he fully intended to use.

It was to be a futile journey. The young man had become seriously ill after leaving Emily and had died from a chest complaint. Emily's plight was now even more serious. Her father decided that the shame was too great to bear and disowned her. She was without a home and, for several months, lived where pity allowed and it was only the birth of the child that brought about a reconciliation. Emily gave birth to a son who took the surname of Barker and was reared by the family. After settling into her role as an unmarried mother, Emily was content to let the tongues cease to wag, and young Tom grew from baby to schoolboy. Tom Barker was to become my grandfather.

Further events in the village of Ipstones led to a disaster for the Johnson family. Jim Johnson, a local lad, had married young but was nevertheless delighted when his wife declared that not only was she pregnant but that twins were a distinct possibility. Delight turned to tragedy when, within the space of a month, Jim became a father and a widower. The tragic death of Jim's wife shocked the village and as is often the case in a small self-contained community, Ipstones embraced Jim and his tragedy.

Time and village support helped Jim to come to terms with life and among those who helped to heal his wounds was Emily Barker. Over the years their friendship blossomed. Affection turned to love and, although Jim was six years younger than Emily, she had no hesitation in accepting his proposal.

The marriage, by all accounts, was a grand affair with Emily wearing a beautiful grey outfit. She was given away by Rowland and the village turned out en masse both at the church and at the reception where Sarah, a girl who had been purchased by Emily's father at a local hire fair, attended the revellers. Sarah, content with her lot, remained with the Barkers for the rest of her life.

Jim, who had previously worked for Thomas Boltons at Froghall now found better prospects on offer at Brittains Paper Mills at Cheddleton. The four mile daily walk from Ipstones to Cheddleton quickly lost its appeal in inclement weather and Jim and Emily sought more convenient accommodation.

Buying number 1 Landsdown Terrace must have been a dream come true. The terraced house with its garden and orchard was in an ideal spot, just a few minutes walk from the paper mills. The garden and orchard were to prove invaluable in later years. Although Jim received a meagre pension when he retired from Brittains it was far from adequate and a substantial degree of self sufficiency was the order of the day. Almost as a matter of course a wide array of vegetables were grown to provide basic food throughout the year. For winter, potatoes, carrots and turnips were stored beneath layers of straw and the remains of summer fruits were preserved in air tight jars. The orchard provided apples, pears, damsons and plums which were also preserved. In addition to the garden produce Jim reared chickens which provided both eggs and meat. How he found the energy is hard to imagine especially as in between time he would take me with him to his 'spare-time' job helping out on Sutton's farm overlooking Cheddleton station.

Shortly after the deaths of Jim and Emily the government, with an eye on social experiments in New Zealand, introduced a welfare scheme with old age pensions and a multitude of social and economic benefits that was to change the face of society. Gone was the need to work from cradle to grave. But although the reforms had great advantages they also had their disadvantages. Jim's garden, long the source of toil and reward, fell into neglect. The hens disappeared along with the raspberry canes and the redcurrant bushes. Lawns appeared in their place as working class parents looked forward to a promised prosperity that was slow to come and failed dismally to lift the gloom of post-War Britain.

In some ways Jim and Emily passed away at the right time. They were fine, hard working people who sought favour from no one and were content to make the most of life through honest toil. I thought of them as grandparents although in reality they were my great grand parents. Either way, they gave me the love and affection that is only found in the special bond that exists between the very young and the very old. I cannot pretend that it was anything but a privilege to have been their grandson.

Brittain's Paper Mills about 1930.

1938

1943

Chapter Three
School Days 1940s

The Staffordshire Moorlands are dotted with outbreaks of rock and heather and are bleak even in the height of summer. These rocks, we children were informed, were the southern end of the Pennine Chain which runs along the centre of England conveniently dividing east from west. More locally the stone was referred to as Millstone Grit and it was from this weather resistant and durable stone that many of the village schools were built. The schools, all endowed practically or spiritually to the Church of England, are so similar in architecture that they appear to be the work of a single individual whose life ambition must have been to work himself to a shadow in pursuit of educational equality.

The School — Cheddleton

Geoffrey Fisher

Cheddleton School

The austere and grim appearance of our school was in direct contrast to the carefree and happy life that existed within. The pattern of school life in the 1940s was much the same as that enjoyed by our parents and grandparents, many of whom spent their entire lives in the village. The playground was divided into girls' and boys' areas, by a wall that went from the school building down to the toilets, and they were strategically situated as far away as possible. At 9 o'clock a whistle was blown, and every child stopped what they were doing and awaited the second whistle. On the second whistle we quickly formed a straight line and marched into school through our own special doors marked boys or girls. This took us into the hall where we turned ninety degrees to pass through the cloakrooms. We quickly found our pegs and deposited coats, hats and scarves before emerging once again into the hall to take our places for morning assembly.

This was one of the highlights of the day. The Headmaster, Mr. Hedley, or the Vicar, Mr. Burgess, selected a hymn. Nothing modern or of doubtful origin, but a traditional hymn sung by countless generations of children before. Mr. Burgess invariably chose 'There is a green hill far away' or 'Every morning the red sun'. Mr Hedley's common choice, and one of the children's favourites, was 'All things bright and beautiful'. Whatever the choice, all were sung with great gusto. Inhibited we were not!

After the morning prayer we walked to our classrooms to begin the pattern of learning that was to become the base stone of our lives. A million years later if someone said to me "*seven sevens*", I would automatically reply "*forty nine*". Whatever the rights or wrongs of learning by rote, when we left Cheddleton school, at the age of eleven, we all had a basic knowledge of arithmetic and a reasonable standard of reading and writing. On other occasion we would listen enthralled as Miss Mellor read to us from *Robin Hood* or *Treasure Island*.

We would also go on nature walks down the lanes or along the canal. It seemed that every wild flower in the world had taken root in that pleasant village. Even now I can picture campions, vetch, marsh marigold, violets, wild garlic and ragged robin, all of which thrived on the land free of pesticides and poisons. Is there a more delightful feeling than warm grass and flowers brushing against young legs?

When school ended I usually made my way home through the fields before the long walk to Landsdown Terrace, along Station Road. Occasionally, though, my wanderlust got the better of me. On one occasion I had sat with Stuart Cotterill in class and when school ended at half past three he asked me if I wanted to go home with him. It seemed an excellent idea and without further ado we set off across the grange banks towards Stuart's house.

Stuart lived in a row of terraced cottages which ran parallel to the Caldon Canal. At the front of each house a long, well tended garden ran to the water's edge. From the garden we could watch the long narrow boats that plied their trade between Etruria and Oakamoor. A stocky horse, that must have been bred specifically to pass beneath the low bridges, strained at a long rope as it pulled tons of coal, copper and crockery to the industries that lined the canal. It was the rope that sliced the grass and vegetation on the side of the towpath and gave it the appearance of a well cut lawn. The barges were wondrous things, brightly painted and shiny, and the bargees themselves were a breed of their own, who handed down their craft from one generation to the next, in a way of life that had hardly changed in a hundred years.

Across the road stood the Boat Inn, an old stone-built ale house frequented by the bargees and by locals who were not too concerned about closing time. Ruth Povey, red faced, stout and kindly, was the landlady of this long established venue, and it was Ruth who willingly supplied us with shandy that was ninety percent pop with nine percent bitter and one percent for Ruth. For another 3d we could share a packet of Smiths Potato Crisps which came complete with its own supply of salt in a wad of blue waterproof paper.

As if all this was not enough for a young boy, running in line with the canal was the River Churnet and over the bridge was the railway station. In direct contrast to the murky river, the station was kept in pristine condition. Signal boxes and waiting rooms were immaculate in cream and maroon, platforms were swept and bordered with flowers, and the stationmaster himself was dressed in navy serge with a peaked cap that put him on a par with an admiral of the fleet. The trains were also immaculate. The carriages bore the LMS logo London-Midlands-Scotland, and were coach-painted in maroon, gold and black. They shone. The door handles shone, the windows shone - and reflected a consideration and service that has long since disappeared. As for the engine, it was a joy, a splendid work of heavy

Basford Bridge and Lane.

The Railway Station.

engineering surrounded by steam and smoke, resting on its laurels and giving the occasional snort or hiss as if barely tolerating the delay as passengers climbed aboard.

To my mind Stuart Cotterill was blessed beyond my wildest dreams and for an hour or two I shared his Utopia. It was only the gathering dusk that finally reminded me of home, and home was about a mile away along a tree lined and lonely road. I hastened to beat the fading light and reached home just as the smoke from the oil lamps was beginning to clear.

At that time I lived with my Granny Johnson who had been blind with cataracts for as long as I could remember. Her normal sweet nature had vanished, and I was met with scolding and a shake that was so unlike my granny that I was left feeling distressed and on the verge of tears. I knew what the problem was of course. Granny had been concerned about my absence and was out of her mind with worry. Despite her blindness she led a completely normal life, which included cooking on a range which housed a huge fire in the centre, an oven on the left side and a hot water boiler with a shiny brass tap on the right.

Resting on the hob above the oven was a frying pan full of fried potatoes which Granny had prepared for my tea. Her composure now fully restored, she ruffled my hair and then deposited the fried potatoes onto my plate. I loved fried potatoes and was about to get stuck into them when, to my dismay, I noticed a large black lump in the middle. For once Granny's impediment had got the upper hand. The black lump was a piece of hardened soot about the size of a half crown. It had obviously fallen from the chimney and Granny, without her sight had not the slightest inkling.

It was now my problem for Granny knew everything about me. She expected a clean plate when I finished. Having already upset her by being late home I felt unable to hurt her feelings, or remind her of her blindness. On the other hand I had the problem of the soot. My pause must have alerted her and as she raised her head towards me I responded quickly by pushing my food around my plate. And the soot? I did what any self respecting seven year old would do. Cutting it into several small pieces I added some potato to each one and quickly ate it. Granny never knew. Or at least I don't think so.

In general, life at home was much the same as life at school. Austere! The aftermath of the War presented its own problems. Food rationing and a general shortage of quality goods did little to raise spirits. The one concession, greeted with enthusiasm, was the arrival of the Dandy and the Beano. I learned to read from a combination of Desperate Dan and cow pies, Lord Snooty and Keyhole Kate, plus a whole range of Enid Blyton adventures. Best of all, whenever I could afford it, was Roy of the Rovers.

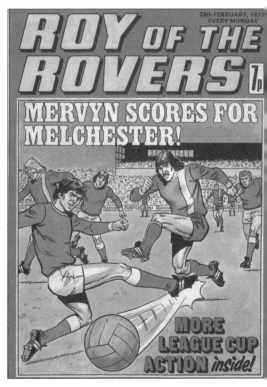

As a footballer Roy was the greatest of all time. A combination of Pele, Eusebio, Stanley Mathews and Gordon Banks. He had a lethal right foot and a left foot that could burst the net. I lost count of the number of times Roy won the cup for Melchester or topped the league, or even saved them from relegation with a last minute goal. Hat tricks were ten a penny and naturally enough he held the club record as the highest goal scorer of all time. Not that Roy limited his talents to goal scoring. He was equally brilliant as winger, half back, full back or goalie and probably marked the pitch out before the match. His greatest attribute was of course his sportsmanship. No dissent or fouling for Roy. Even after the most gruelling game he would crawl the length of the pitch with his broken leg to shake hands with his opposite number - *Well played Jack, great game!"* Time has caught up with Roy but I am pleased to tell you that his most dedicated disciple still sits in Row C, Block H in the main stand. As for Melchester they remain resolute and skilful as ever. As you might expect, they are led by son of Roy, a chip of the old block.

My other hero was also called Roy. He rode a horse called Trigger and I met him on Saturday afternoon at the Palace Cinema in Leek. What a man! Roy Rogers was everything a cowboy should be; slim, tall and handsome and lightening fast on the draw. The films followed a well tried routine. The baddies would rob a bank or the stagecoach and, as the terrified victims fainted or recoiled in horror, Roy and Trigger would gallop to the rescue. Bullets would fly everywhere and a ferocious fist fight with the gang leader finally ended when the leader fell to his death and the others fled. As the dust settled, Roy and Trigger galloped off into the sunset (well Trigger galloped). As he slowly disappeared from view the film turned to sepia as we heard a snatch of the song "A four legged friend, a four legged friend." Not for nothing was he called the singing cowboy. And all without breaking sweat or getting his shirt creased.

It was the cinemas that initially attracted me to Leek and the town had several. The Palace, the Majestic and a rather posh one called the Grand. The cinemas gave good value with a B film, then the Pathe News and finally the main feature. As the final curtain closed, the National Anthem was played as we all stood to attention.

> *And nobody rushed for the door of the hall*
> *As the most stirring Anthem would ring*
> *And all the old soldiers went quiet and stood tall*
> *As the band played God save the King.*

In those days before television the cinema offered the easiest form of escape and, for a while, a mobile cinema visited the Churnet Village Hall each Friday. It was there I watched a wonderful film called 'One Million Years B.C.' and fell in love with a long legged beauty called Raquel Welch. As the dialogue was somewhat limited to prehistoric mumblings with an American accent it has to be said that the film hardly tested her acting ability, but in her flimsy wolf skin costume she performed well enough for most men to award her an Oscar. It has to be said that later versions of that film never did seem quite the same.

Even better that the films were the dances. I would sneak onto the balcony that overlooked the crowded floor and watch as the local sophisticates danced in time to the music and obeyed the calls of the Master of Ceremonies, occasionally adding an impromptu twirl to impress. As the night wore on, passion and beer took hold and the dancing became more and

more boisterous. The Lancers and the Gay Gordons had everyone on their feet as even th
wallflowers began to feel confident. Steps and decorum were forgotten, the sophisticate
tutted but joined in as everyone went mad for a few minutes as the midnight hour approached
In the midst of it all my sisters made the most of it as the lights were lowered for the goodnigh
kiss, and as I walked home I could hear the rustling as the more adventuresome snogged unde
the canal bridge, and the last strains of the band and the singer crooned:

> *On a warm summer night*
> *When our fancy took flight*
> *And the music was lively and gay.*
> *Then as Johnny Pitt sang*
> *His song with the band*
> *We danced in the old fashioned way.*

Even in those days of perpetual summer the weekends passed all too quickly and I foun
myself once again back at school. The walk to school took about thirty minutes; down Statio
Road, along the main road to the canal then a short cut up the steep fields towards the churc
and the Black Lion; then just a few hundred yards more to the Top School on Park Lane.

At the beginning of term we were greeted by the dentist for an oral examination and the
by the nit nurse who examined us everywhere else, including our heads. Nits thrived i
Cheddleton. When one child had nits we all had nits. We were told that nits thrived on clea
heads and this left me totally baffled as we were told to scrub our heads anyway. In betwee
scrubbings I had to sit with my head over a piece of the News Chronicle whilst my Grann
Barker painstakingly combed my hair with a fine tooth metal comb. I could hear the nits a
they dropped onto the newspaper as the comb dragged its way over my scalp. Finally I wa
taken to the sink where a thick white solution called Suleo was massaged into my hair. It lef
my head stinging and nit free - until the next time.

Even worse than Suleo was the humiliation suffered by some of the boys in my class
These boys simply had their heads shaved all over except for a short fringe that remained a
the front and made them look even more odd. My heart went out to them as they huddle
together in a corner of the school yard. One or two boys made remarks but most of us coul
have wept for them as they stood like convicts with nowhere to go.

Some days I could not wait to escape but my freedom and adventures had to take secon
place to education. As time progressed we began to take our class examinations whic
culminated in a report that gave marks and comments for individual subjects, a total mark an
our position in class. Whichever class I was in I remained in sixth position. I never achieve
anything remotely like top marks for arithmetic but managed to obtain excellent results i
composition and poetry, which stood me in great stead when I worked as a maintenance fitter

As we neared the age of eleven the intensity of tests and examinations increased. W
were approaching the end of our time at the village school and our futures depended ver
much on whether we continued our education at the grammar school, or the secondary moder
school, in Leek. Our success, or lack of it, depended on our result in the 11-plus examinatio
an event that sorted out the wheat from the chaff. I was destined to be with the chaff!

For months before, our class took mock examinations based on past exam papers. W
could hardly have been better prepared and that particular year proved to be a good one fo

most schools. The result was a shortage of places at the grammar school and some stringent marking. It worked well enough and the brightest members of our class were granted places. As for me, I was a border line case and this meant attending an interview with the headmaster at Leek High School who would make the final decision.

I remember standing in front of this formidable person who wore long black robes and asked me a number of the strangest questions. Just as I began to get confident, he said *"Tell me Alan, from where you are standing, where is the North Point?"* What's the North Point, I thought. In for a penny in for a pound, I looked out of his study window and said *"It's over there."* He gave me a look that he obviously kept just for imbeciles. *"No Alan, it is directly opposite to where you pointed."* So ended my brush with academia and also those days at my delightful junior school.

On my final day, when school had ended, instead of leaving immediately I wandered back into the hall to find my mates. I found them all hanging around waiting for Mr. Hedley who promptly came out of his class and asked us all to line up. He then, very solemnly shook each pupil by the hand, wished them all well and gave us a last bit of advice regarding our careers. He shook hands with David Maskery. *"You should go in for mathematics David."* To David Pegg he advised building, or architecture. To someone else he advised teaching. As I approached the front of the queue I envisaged great and noble futures for all my friends. My turn at last came; what would he advise? He paused for a few moments, then shaking me firmly by the hand he said, *"Alan, I think you should do something with your hands."* As I made my way, somewhat deflated, to the door I thought, *"cheeky sod."*

York Railway Museum

A LMS carrier in Cheddleton - a frequent sight around the village.

LMS Railway

London, Midlands, Scotland, running true to time,
Delivering goods to Brittains on the Churnet Valley line.
Buckets for the farmers in stainless or enamel
Delivered by Les Johnson in a three-wheeled Scammel.

Familiar smell of damp and smoke
The fireman shovelling coal and coke,
Familiar sounds of hissing steam
Belies the engine black and clean.

A train of endless carriages filled with wood and steel,
Pulled forever forward on huge reluctant wheels,
From Uttoxeter and Alton, through Cheddleton and Leek
Filled to overflowing on Wednesday every week.

Familiar smells of damp and smoke
The fireman shovelling coal and coke,
Familiar sounds of hissing steam
Belies the engine black and clean.

Resplendent in its livery of gold, maroon and black
Borne proudly by the driver and guardsman at the back
London, Midland, Scotland running true to time,
Through the glory that is England, the Churnet Valley Line.

Denstone to Oakamoor Railway Line (Disused)

Where Cellandine and Primrose in wild abundance grow
And the brambles are a tangle with the matted undergrowth
Where the Dog Tooth Violet shyly peeps from underneath trees
And the fragrance of the Bluebells comes drifting on the breeze.

Where the ambling rambling river ignores the shortest route
And a Robin starts a singing and the others follow suit
Where the Willow dangles branches towards the gentle flow
and the Coots are busy building on the muddy banks below.

Where occasionally we encounter the influence of men,
An iron bridge, a rampart, a platform now and then.
Where a wary rabbit freezes and eyes us as we pass
And cautious, ever cautious, continues nibbling at the grass.

Until at last the eager walkers espy the Ramblers Retreat
And head for Keelings tables where they rest their weary feet.
Until again the green woods beckon, they leave the café door
To walk through Beech-clad woodland, enroute to Oakamoor.

Geofrey Fisher

Basil Jeuda

Cheddleton Railway Station.
Left: The last two stationmasters.

1946

1946

1947

1947

STAFFORDSHIRE EDUCATION COMMITTEE.

CHEDDLETON CHURCH OF ENGLAND SCHOOL.

Report for Term ending 21 Dec. 1949

Name Alan Gibson　　Age 11 3/12　　Class III A

Position in Class 6　　Number in Class 26　　Mark Good

Attendance : Absent 6

Late —　　　　　Conduct Satisfactory

Subject	Actual Marks	Possible	Teacher's Report
Mech. Arith.	34	50	
Mental Arith.	19	20	
MATHEMATICS Problems	22	50	
READING	18	20	Alan is improving
COMPOSITION	16	20	and making steady
~~LITERATURE~~ ENGLISH	33	40	progress.
RECITATION	20	20	Inclined to hurry in
~~HISTORY~~ SCRIPTURE	18	20	his work and this leads
GEOGRAPHY	17	20	to mistakes which could
~~HYGIENE~~ SPELLING	13	20	be avoided with greater
NATURE STUDY ~~OR SCIENCE~~	19	20	care
DRAWING PAINTING	13	20	
PASTEL	12	20	
DESIGN	17	20	
Craftwork	20	20	
Writing & Neatness	18	20	
	309	400	

Class Teacher

Head Teacher J N Hedley

Ray Poole

A view from Bridge Eye.

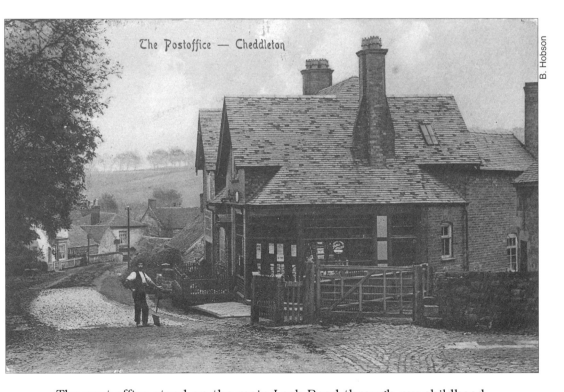

B. Hobson

The post office stood on the main Leek Road through my childhood.

Two old postcards of Cheddleton Church, above, viewed from Park Lane,
and below the fine reredos and lectern.

**The following three pages are photographs of
Cheddleton School classes in the early 1930s.**

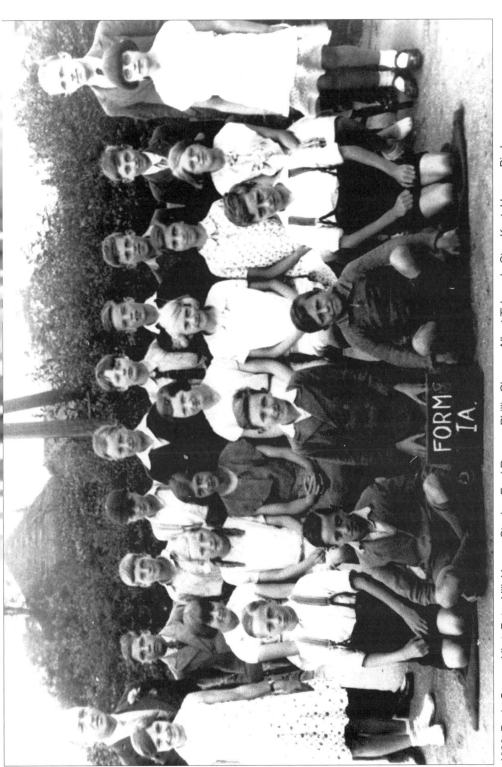

1930: Back: George Hirst, Peter Hill, Horace Stanley, Fred Rogers, Phillip Clowes, Albert Tidmarsh, Stan Kent, Horace Birch
Middle: Nancy Hood, Joan Barker, Winifred Sleigh, Doreen Berresford, Betty Clifford, Selina Duffield, Beryl Forrester, Annie Hammond, Nellie Finney
Front: Ray Birley, Gordon Hill, Keith Raine, Doug Spooner, Jack Kent. Standing, Left, Mr Goodwin; Right, Mr Hedley.

1932: Back: Eric Johnson, Don Sutton, Bill Hammond, Harold Berresford, Bernard Whittaker, Ernie Clowes
Middle: Mary Eardley, Betty Alcock, Miriam Childs, Irene Nicholls, Mary Waine, Gladys Fisher, Gladys Hanley, Joan Saunders
Seated: Lena Dainty, Louise Ellams, Hilda Hanley, Joyce Jones, Eileen Ramshaw
Sitting on ground: Harry Pegg, Lawrence Clowes, Alf Spooner. Standing, left Mr Goodwin; right, Mr Hedley

Evacuees at Caverswall

Chapter Four
A Surrogate Sister

It may be stating the obvious, but the people of Cheddleton were not really familiar with the dramatic changes that occurred in Germany during the 1930s. Hitler's rise from obscurity and his success in turning a financially devastated nation into a thriving industrial concern was enough to sweep him to the pinnacle of political power. A few politicians expressed unease at his programme of reform and urged the government to exercise caution. These warnings were, for the most part, ignored, but plans had been considered in 1938 for the evacuation of major cities in the event of war. Experiences in the recent Spanish wars had demonstrated only too clearly the consequences of the mass bombing on urban areas and, for once, Britain was prepared. Or almost.

When war was declared in September of 1939 the evacuation of women and children from the major cities to the safe retreat of the countryside became an urgent priority. On the other hand the Country was now at war and the embarkation of troops was also an urgent priority. The result was a mass of humanity moving to various destinations on trains and buses that were simply unable to cope with such numbers. The planned 'Pied Piper' excursion became a nightmare as people were misdirected, lost or left behind.

Amongst the most urgent cases were the children of North London with its factories, housing estates and working class population. In the course of time North London, East London and the docks were to suffer horrendous damage as the Luftwaffe discharged ton after ton of bombs and incendiaries on the capital.

In 1939 it was the home of Cecil Hanrahan and his wife Mary whose memories of County Sligo and Dublin were still fresh in their minds. In the country of their adoption they worked hard to improve their lot and to raise a young family in the Catholic traditions of their faith. The poverty of Southern Ireland had been replaced by the regular income Cecil earned as a car sprayer and the little luxuries of life were provided by Mary who had found employment in Marks and Spencer's Highbury store. The three children, Gerald, Mary and Shirley, attended the Catholic School where they were cared for by the Sisters of Our Lady of the Sacred Hearts convent.

The decision to evacuate must have been very hard indeed but in those first weeks of September several million people moved from the cities to rural destinations all over Britain. Within a few months many had returned again to their homes rather than face an uncertain future with strangers and unfamiliar surroundings. Those that remained suffered mixed fortunes. Some found the countryside appealing and settled happily with caring local families. Others, to their dismay, were ill treated and abused and longed to return home.

The mix of children, rich and poor, healthy or diseased, exacerbated the problem. Head lice, impetigo and scabies spread like wildfire as youngsters travelled to distant villages and arrived looking frightened, sorrowful and close to tears. The nuns of Our Lady of the Sacred Hearts accompanied their charges onto the train, and the Hanrahans and the other children, clutching carrier bags and gas masks, set off for an unknown and an uncertain future. Why the train headed for Cromer is beyond comprehension. Whether a simple mistake or a change of plan, or whatever, the children arrived several hours later in the seaside town where their reception caused a great deal of confusion and a rapid decision to house them overnight before putting them back on the train. This time their journey took them to North Staffordshire. First of all to temporary accommodation in Caverswall and then on to Cheddleton where they assembled in the Churnet Hall.

They were greeted by a reception committee consisting of the Women's Institute, the W.V.S. and local councillors. After a brief rest and refreshments the group were marched, with their meagre possessions, along Station Road. They stopped at various houses where the occupants had agreed to billet the evacuees. One by one they were examined and either accepted or rejected, if their face did or did not fit.

Eventually the apprehensive group arrived outside Granny Barker's and awaited inspection. Granny made her choice, just one child who looked up with alarm at the nuns. A brief discussion revealed the problem. The child was part of a family group who were to remain together. Granny made her second choice. Her eyes settled on the smallest member of the group and four year old Shirley Hanrahan found herself a welcome member of our young family. There was no room for the other Hanrahans. Gerald was lodged with the Garbetts and later with the Chells who lived on Basford Bridge Lane. Mary and Patsy Judge were billeted with the Clemsons who lived in a small bungalow farther along Station Road and close to the Churnet Valley railway line.

Mary Hanrahan was still suffering the after effects of meningitis and was taken to Cheadle to the cottage hospital. Gerald Hanrahan, the eldest child, remained with the Chells for two years until he reached the age of eleven when he was transferred to Surrey. The Hanrahans were to remain apart until 1946 and Cecil and Mary made endless trips to Cheddleton, Cheadle and Surrey in an effort to keep in touch with their children.

As for Shirley, her formative years were spent in the bosom of Granny Barker who reared her as one of her own. She was so much an integral part of our family that I genuinely thought she was my sister. We shared the pains and pleasures of growing up with a kind and generous woman.

Being just four years of age meant Shirley had almost a year to settle and to get used to our ways before starting school. And school turned out to be a problem. Shirley was a Catholic and the village was simply not prepared for such diversions. Heretics, heathens, even Methodists were tolerated. But Catholics! My God! What on earth could we do with them? The answer in Shirley's case was a mixture of venues which ranged from a daily trip to Cheadle or Leek, a spell at Cheddleton school and temporary classrooms in the Churnet Hall. As for Sundays and Mass, St. Edward's was out of the question. Even family weddings were frowned upon for a young Catholic. Quite how the village elders came to terms with the Black Lion is anyone's guess but that is where a limited Catholic service was held each Sunday under the guidance of a priest from Leek and the Landlady Betty Weller.

Education and religion apart, Shirley's memories are remarkably happy and mirror our own memories closely. The village fetes with the band playing 'Blaze Away', the smell of fruits and vegetables in the marquees and the parade of the carnival queen, remain to this day. As might be expected visits to the village shops were a pleasure to be savoured. Bold's store, Mr Grainger at the Post Office, Ted Ede the Cobbler and Mr Gayes who made the most wonderful bread imaginable.

Even pinching coal, Bobby Lord not withstanding, remains a vivid memory. Coal was always in short supply during the war years and we children were quick to join the others 'tidying up'! after the bargees had delivered coal to Brittains boiler house by the canal tow path. Not that our efforts were always appreciated - especially when Shirley managed to confuse the coal with large lumps of black stone which we humped all the way back to Landsdown Terrace.

It was not all subversive activity. No doubt Shirley would have been drummed out of Brownies had Miss Starling, the Brown Owl, been aware of her clandestine affairs. Instead she thrived on a diet of knot tying, fire lighting and tracking. She even met Lady Baden Powell on one of her rare visits to Leek.

This was life then with the Barkers. Christmas with its simple presents and home-made decorations, carol singing and the general excitement and anticipation that always bore fruit. Bonfire night when almost every road had a huge fire with blackened roast potatoes, was an annual ritual not to be missed, as was the harvest gathering. The pleasures of the fruit and corn gathering gained an added significance when all the children took baskets to school. Each basket was decorated with coloured crepe or tissue paper before being filled with the products of the village harvest. Apples, pears, plums and damsons fought for space with greengage, red currants, black currants and raspberries, before the overflowing baskets were blessed at the church and then borne by the pupils to every pensioner in the village. We were really proud on that day and the old folk, usually so independent, played their part by making us especially welcome and keeping up a tradition that had existed since the beginning of time.

The schools also taught the practicalities of life. If Shirley had no socks to darn Granny simply cut a hole in one and despatched her to school complete with bobbin, needle and wool. Miss Clews patiently ensured that each child produced a neat weave that left the stocking looking as good as new.

We had our holidays, of course, and trips to Rudyard Lake, the pantomime at Hanley and a train ride to Alton Towers gardens competed with the Sunday School trip by barge to Consall, with a stop for sandwiches and pop at a canal side pub.

Even the seriousness of the war escaped us as we went about our simple pleasures. The army lorries that struggled to beat the incline of Wall Lane Bank were seen as an opportunity rather than a symbol of war. The secret was to run behind the lorries shouting "any gum chum?" The Americans were always generous and chocolate, fruit and cocoa accompanied the chewing gum that was thrown from the back of the lorries.

Other aspects of war also intruded from time to time. German planes would fly down the Churnet Valley occasionally in an effort to find the copper works at Oakamoor and, on one occasion, Leek became an unexpected target. We were told that a bomb had been dropped on a building next to Britannia Street School, opposite the Palace cinema. If Hitler thought he had problems with Britain he should have been grateful that the 'Palace' remained intact. Had that not been the case we kids would have attacked Germany en-masse. We knew where our priorities lay.

The same can be said about Granny Barker. Her indignity came to the fore in no uncertain terms when Shirley's uncle was arrested. Granny said "It was a bit of a bugger" and I suppose it was really. We knew Shirley's family were a bit religious, what with mass and going to church all the time. We also realised it was going to be a hard job turning her into a heretic, but calling her uncle a spy was a bit much; just because he was a monk. In actual fact Shirley's uncle, Dan Hanrahan, was a member of the Franciscan order and was known to his friends as Brother Fideles. Dan had arrived in Cheddleton with Cecil Hanrahan on one of his visits to see his children. By coincidence, the radio had announced details of a monk who had been at large for some time and was suspected of taking photographs of industrial sites which were then used by German bombers to pin point their targets.

And suddenly, there was Dan, strolling casually along the canal by Brittain's Paper Mills deep in conversation with Cecil. This was a golden opportunity for the police and the Home Guard to show their metal. As Dan and Cecil approached the locks they were apprehended and placed under arrest. Amidst a great deal of excitement the pair were taken to the Churnet Hall for interrogation. It was easy enough for Cecil to prove his identity. He had visited often enough and anyway Granny Barker said he was all right.

Dan had to suffer a while longer before Cecil and Granny could convince everyone of his innocence. It was getting quite close to tea time in the end so they had to let him go; Granny Barker didn't like anyone being late for tea.

So our Shirley left her mark. With her Southern accent, spying and mass every day it was a wonder we could turn her into our sister, but turn her we did. So much so that a picture remains forever in my mind's eye. It is 1946 and Mary Hanrahan has come to collect her daughter. This lady whom I vaguely knew had appeared wearing a smart coat and a fashionable hat. As I stand at the gate the lady walks away, a suitcase in one hand and Shirley in the other. What is happening to Shirley? Why are they taking her away? I was eight years old, Shirley was being taken away from me and I felt totally inadequate.

Hollow Lane.

Wall Lane.

Looking from the Tanyard area towards the canal.

Main Road.

The Canal Bridge.

Chapter Five
A Cheddleton Childhood

The road that leads to Basford and Ipstones must once have been as pleasant as any in the village. Until the industrial revolution came along and changed it that is. Those first changes came towards the end of the eighteenth century when a local Quaker family, fighting the bigotry of the time, took one of the few options open to them. They did the job no one else wanted and opened a tannery close to where our road joined the Leek road. Life being down to earth in those days, the area immediately became known as the skin-yard.

From this beginning the industry of Cheddleton began to spread along the valley of the River Churnet and of greater significance was the growth of paper making. The initial venture to produce hand-made paper had begun in a field called Butchers Meadow and it was there, on the banks of the river, that the village nurtured what was to become Britain's Paper Mills, a company which at its height employed almost one thousand people and had world-wide fame.

In the 19th century a railway line was constructed from North-Rode to Uttoxeter. The Churnet Valley Line running through countryside of breath-taking beauty, had a station at Cheddleton which opened up a whole new world for the villagers. Our road had reached the point of no return and, in keeping with the changes, someone had the inspirational idea of calling it Station Road.

And so it was that, instead of spending my early years in a small cottage on an idyllic country lane, I came to spend my time at Number 1, Landsdown Terrace, Station Road, Cheddleton. By the time my story begins a second world war was raging in Europe and Brittain's Paper Mills had spread for almost a mile along the flat meadow land that lay between the River Churnet and Station Road.

Landsdown Terrace was one of a number of terraces that had been built in the early part of the twentieth century. Most of these houses were occupied by the families who depended on the paper mills for their livelihood. My great grandparents, Jim and Emily Johnson, occupied number one and my grandparents, Tom and Martha Barker, lived in number five. Another of my grandparents, Bill Gibson, lived nearby on Higgers Hill. All worked at the paper mills for most of their lives.

Bill Gibson, after the First World War, spent a few years in his native Burslem before he too joined the paper mill, where he remained for thirty seven years. Through his efforts he reached the heady heights of yard foreman with around fifty men under his supervision and was reponsible for all the external building and building repair works around the works. for this his salary never exceeded £5.00 per week. Even so he managed to keep his wife and family, run a small car and buy his terraced house. And on his death he was able to leave we grandchildren a few thousand pounds each.

How we came to live at Number One is outside my memory, although I know that we lived with the Johnsons, my great grandparents, for some time, and, when they passed away, my parents were left with a free house and some very fine furniture. Tables inlaid with rose wood and mahogany, balloon back chairs, bureaus and inlaid tables for chess and board games. In the parlour were the large chairs and sofa reserved for Sundays and special occasions. Also in that room was the very large black bible with its maps of Palestine and a picture of Jesus sitting with his disciples at the last supper - all looking at a glum faced Judas who, no doubt, wished he was at home counting his thirty pieces of silver.

Outside the house the growth of the paper mills continued unabated and with it the stench from the effluent, the waste product that was left after the paper making process was completed. This effluent flowed into absorbent canals and eventually settled opposite the houses in Station Road. The stench from the muck pools, as we called them, perfused the country air for a good distance around. It certainly reached Number One - it filtered into every nook and cranny of our existence.

It was a very ordinary house consisting of a kitchen, a living room and a parlour. A steep flight of stairs led to two main bedrooms and a box room that overlooked the wash house and the earth closet. It was the box room that I occupied, my little body fitting well enough into the large hollow where the flock mattress had sunk to the floor between the broken springs. That bed was a forerunner of things to come. Any decent furniture in the house began to disappear as buyers, ever eager for quality at bargain prices, provided my parents with the money for survival. The parlour was stripped bare until only the oil lamp hanging from its central hook and the linoleum remained. In the living room we were left with a robust plain table, four shabby chairs and a three piece suite that was slowly but surely dropping to pieces.

On a small table by the stairs stood an old wireless that had seen better days and challenged our efforts to tune into radio Luxembourg and the top twenty. The kitchen was even more basic. A painted dresser, grubby and dilapidated, stood by the wall. Opposite was the shallow brown sink or slopstone above which stood the single tap that supplied cold water for drinking, washing, cooking and cleaning. Bathroom and toilets were something we saw in magazines and certainly not for the likes of us. To wash we took our turn at the sink; one brother, myself, and two sisters battling for a block of hard carbolic soap which was reluctant to lather under the cold water. A worn towel hung from a nail on the door. As often as not a swift wipe with a flannel had to suffice, or a brisk rub with the towel. It became a standing joke between the four of us that if we couldn't have a wash at least we could have a good dry!

I have no doubt many people in the village suffered hardship and poverty during and after the War. It was only as we got old enough to notice and compare that I realised just how poor we were. I envied the boys who had proper shoes and wore ties and jumpers. We shrugged it off of course. We learned to hide the frustration and tears when our pathetic efforts to improve our lot came to nothing. The common cause whilst not quite "first up best dressed" made us sharp enough to survive the pecking order. A blasphemous retort or a humorous quip were part of our survival package, our way of coping with an adult world we neither liked nor understood. And with our parents it was a case of "out of sight, out of mind". We did our best to comply by disappearing for hour after hour. We knew every field and every road in the village and, when my sisters tired of my company, I wandered alone. My loneliness and lack of affection paradoxically provided me with my greatest friends as, in my mind, I daydreamed of a life full of happiness. In my dreamland my stomach was always full, my parents were happy and life was worth living. The reality was somewhat different. The laughter between the misery took me from the depths of despair to the height of ecstasy and back again.

The austerity of our lives was matched by the primitive conditions that surrounded us. The tin bath and the closet represented my worst nightmares. The bath was kept outside when not in use and hung by its handle from a six inch nail that my father had hammered into the wall. The closet was at the top of the yard and it stunk to high heaven in warm weather, when it was home to a swarm of flies, woodlice and earwigs. In the midst of it all I sat on the rough wooden board drumming my feet to discourage the insects and whistling Danny Boy to discourage intruders. Our toilet paper consisted of last week's copy of the Radio Times which had been cut into quarters and now hung from a nail on the wall. My father was good with nails!

Going to the closet during the night was even worse. Our only means of illumination was the candle. On such occasions I would creep down the stairs in my shirt trying desperately not to waken everyone and thus engaging the wrath of my father or a shriek of hysterical laughter from my mother. One night I reached the kitchen and fumbled in the drawer for a saucer, a candle and some matches. Having lit the candle I melted some wax and let it form a small pool in the saucer. Into this pool of hot wax I stuck the candle and allowed it to set. This was the easy bit. I now had to get from the kitchen, across the yard and into the closet. Putting the candle down I gently opened the back door and a blast of cold air immediately blew out the candle. After several attempts I decided that moonlight was my only option, except that their was no moon. The night was as black as pitch as I stepped out of the door and groped my way forward. Fumbling my way past the rain tub I finally made it. I was quick if nothing else and, after a quick wipe on housewife's choice, I set about my return journey. By now my imagination was running riot and I made the fatal error of rushing. In doing so I forgot the tin bath. I hit it full on and it fell from the wall with a clatter that would awaken the dead. The sound reverberated for what seemed an age before finally settling to a gentle rattle. I picked up the bath and, after several attempts, managed to put it back on the nail. I waited for the reaction: not a sound was heard. My heart pounded as I crept back upstairs. I had got away with it! No good-hiding. No shouting at. I blissfully returned to my slumbers.

The following morning I had my wash, then, with my hands in my pockets, I walked casually into the yard to check on the bath. As I did so I heard footsteps and glanced towards the gate. Percy Shenton, our next door neighbour, was going past. "Good morning Alan," he said. "Morning Mr. Shenton," I said. He paused and looked towards me, "Do me a favour will you Alan." "What's that Mr. Shenton?" I replied. "In future if you want to visit the closet can you do it before midnight."

The bath came into its own on Friday night. Bath night was a treat not to be missed. The bath was placed in front of the living room fire, usually in Granny Barker's house at Number Five. Hot water from the fireside boiler, plus endless kettles, gradually filled the bath to about one third full. Then, with no hint of shyness, we all undressed and awaited our turn to follow each other into the water. Just occasionally I would be first in and for a few minutes I could soak while the aroma of carbolic soap and Dettol wafted around my skinny body. Then it was a thorough washing followed by a brisk drying in front of the fire. All quite wonderful if you were the first one. For the rest, the water got murkier and murkier and the towels got wetter and wetter as the ritual progressed.

When we were not battling to wash we were battling to eat. My staple diet consisted of porridge, beans on toast, chips and bread and jam. The porridge, with a generous helping of black treacle, gave me a stomach like lead but only served to stave off the hunger until lunch time. Chips were everyone's favourite and if we could add an egg or some Spam we were well pleased. Several rounds of bread and butter helped to fill the gap. (It was margarine from the Co-Op really but I liked to swank). For the most part I was more interested in the quantity of the food than the quality. As often as not a feast or a famine situation prevailed. Immediately any food arrived we promptly ate it all. To hell with tomorrow, eat it while it's there was our philosophy. The famines came often enough and, as our stomachs rumbled, we learned to scavenge. Potatoes and carrots from the fields, apples from the orchards. When those supplies were exhausted the scraps saved for the pig man were fair game.

One winter's night Wendy and I sat in front of a dwindling fire contemplating our supper. A quick search of the cupboards and the pantry revealed nothing. Except for the usual tins and cooking essentials the cupboard was well and truly bare. Mother had even forgotten the bread. In desperation we turned to the brown carrier bag that held the pig food. I lifted it off its nail (I told you Dad was good with nails) and rummaged through the scraps. By now my Mother and Wendy were helpless with laughter, but my luck was in, for there, at the very bottom, was a rock solid crust, a whole slice of bread. The bread was speckled with bluish grey spots where the mould had started to grow. We looked at each other and then at the bread. "See if it will scrape off," urged Wendy. So with a few deft strokes of the knife I scraped away the mould and passed it to her. With the crust now skewered onto the end of our long wire toasting fork she held it in front of the embers whilst it turned each side to a lovely golden brown. A liberal coating of margarine and the feast was complete. I took a first tentative mouthful and closed my eyes in ecstasy. It tasted absolutely wonderful; my half slice never touched the sides.

To be fair it was not all sadness and hunger. We had our friends and the traditional games, many of which were seasonal. Cricket, rounders, hopscotch and running in the summer; football, conkers and marbles in the winter. Conkers involved not only playing the game but collecting, storing and hardening the horse chestnuts. To harden the conkers we steeped them in vinegar for a few days then baked them in the oven. The result was a lump of shriveled up chestnut with which you hoped to annihilate every other conker in sight.

Len Hutton

The two favourites for me were always football and cricket. I practised long and hard to emulate my heroes. Stanley Matthews and Dixie Dean, or Dennis Compton, Cyril Washbrook and Len Hutton. Our sports arena was a straight piece of road between our house and the Alcock's. The Alcock family had played cricket for Ashcombe Park for generations and a bat and ball were always available. The cricket would last all day, mostly with me and my mates bowling at Stan Alcock. Being a little older than the rest of us he was by far the best cricketer. His wicket was the most prized and we tried everything to remove him. Leg spin, off spin, fast, slow, googlies and chinamen. All were treated with disdain and smashed out of sight. When we eventually bowled him we were so knackered that our own stay at the wicket was short-lived.

As always in life the wheel of fortune turns and we were greeted one day with the news that Stan was going away. He had received his call up papers for National Service. Not only was he to enlist in the army he was also going to war. Roger announced that Stan was going to Korea. "Korea! Where's Korea?" I asked. We looked at each other with blank expressions. "Will he be able to come home at night?" I asked. "I don't think so," said Roger. "Bloody hell," I thought, "It must be north of Hanley then."

At this point the light dawned as we realised that Stan would no longer dominate the game. This was great news. We knew it would not be for long. Stan would soon sort things out, win a few medals and then return. In the meantime he was out of the way and that night I thought a quick prayer was justified. "Now God. Stan is going away for a bit. But I know him, he will be back in no time. This is a golden opportunity to sort him out once and for all. I know he is my mate but he is a bloody nuisance with that bat. Do you think he can be injured a bit? Nothing too serious, a club foot or a withered hand will do. As long as it impairs his ability with the bat. OK God. I'll leave it with you. Oh - and can he win a medal as well?"

With that I fell into a contented sleep. Fortune had smiled upon me and I dreamed of filling Stan's shoes. A couple of birthdays passed but that wheel kept on turning and before I knew where I was we had news of Stan's pending return. I had just smashed John Lovatt's leg spin into Turner's garden when a familiar figure came round the corner. With a kit bag on his shoulder, holding his medals I thought, Stan's face lit up and he lengthened his stride. Throwing the bag to one side he asked for the bat. First John Lovatt bowled him out, then Roger, then myself. It was easy. he had simply lost his timing. "I need some practice lads," he said. " I'll be back" and with that he picked up the kit bag and went into his house. I knew who he would be practising with and as I watched him run up the path to his mum and dad I realised that God had failed me once again. He didn't even limp!

I could also watch Stan and my sisters perform at the Churnet Hall, the large cavernous building that stood on the banks of the Caldon Canal. The Churnet Hall was the venue for almost all village activities. Whist drives, youth clubs, cinema, dances, triumphs and disasters, all were part of life's pattern. It was the place where grown-ups enjoyed themselves and where I was not allowed. I went nevertheless. On pictures night we watched Abbot and Costello, Frank Randle, Old Mother Riley and a host of black and white films which were but a few steps removed from the silent movies and Pearl White. All it lacked was the organ rising from the bowels of the hall.

The dances and the films were weekly events but even these took second place when the annual carnival came around. Over the years the carnival raised thousands of pounds for charity and it was the job of each carnival queen not only to raise money, but to outdo the previous year's collection. What pressures this put on the unfortunate parents I dread to think, but it did not stop the young girls of the village from applying for the royal status. My closest brush with this royalty came the year Rosalie Shenton became queen. There was talk of the need for a page boy and certain eyes were cast in my direction. I could actually feel myself dying on the spot and, although I was never much of a believer, I resorted again to prayer and 'Alleluia', it worked. I would never have raised my head again. Me - a page boy!

For some reason beyond comprehension the carnival was held at the bottom of a steep

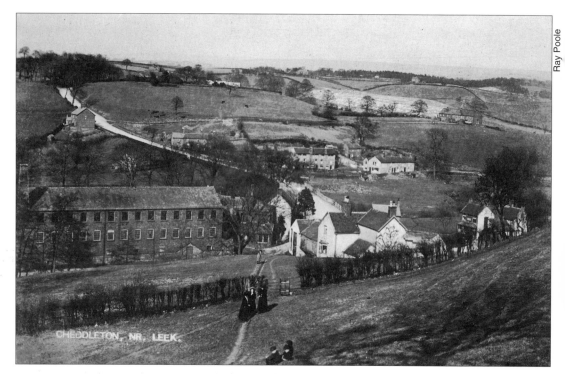

Ray Poole

Churnet Hall, Cheddleton.

hill in one of Steel's fields, just beyond the railway station. A long parade began in the village and made its way along Station Road. The queens paraded on decorated floats, open-backed lorries complete with satin seats, banners and streamers. At the head sat the young queen, dressed for the occasion and all around her sat her retinue who waved regally at the crowd.

Visiting queens from the far flung villages of Ipstones, Alton, Bagnall, Wetley Rocks and Endon made up the colourful procession whilst, at the head of it all, strode the Cheddleton Silver Band. The band were quite splendid as they oompahed their way along the road in a cacophony of trombones, cornets, pipes and drums, gloriously out of step and lost in the rhythm of a great day.

Reaching the field at last I joined my mates and astutely avoided the crowning ceremony with its long winded speeches and beaming parents. There were races to be run and greasy poles to climb, ice creams and candy floss and most important of all, sideshows with coconuts, goldfish and earthenware ornaments to be won. At the end of it all I wandered back to Landsdown Terrace clutching a jam jar of water in which a bewildered goldfish swam around and around wondering how the hell I had managed to draw the short straw.

Getting to Leek was an adventure in itself. First I saved the money earned from helping Grand-dad Barker deliver the Sunday papers. Then with money to burn I would await the following Wednesday or Saturday. I had the choice of three buses; PMT - Potteries Motor Traction, Procters and Berresfords. PMT were by far the most superior. They were clean, mechanically sound and punctual. They were also soulless and indifferent. Proctors occupied the middle ground, whilst Berresfords came a poor third in efficiency, but first by a mile in terms of friendliness and convenience.

Berresfords were everything a bus company should not be. Unpunctual, unsound and

Mrs R. Salmon

Carnival Queen
Glenys Tatton, Rosalie
Shenton and Joyce
Shenton.

Rosalie Shenton and
her attendants.

Mrs R. Salmon

Berresford's Motors
1920s to 1970s

R.N. Ogden

R.N. Ogden

R.N. Ogden

M. Berresford

R.N. Ogden

M. Berresford

noisy and as often as not encased in a shroud of black smoke. We loved them. Berresfords were the ones who waited for the late comers, who made sure you got home at night and would never, never, have dreamt of leaving a young child stranded or alone. All the buses had a precise number of passengers that they were allowed to carry but for some reason this did not concern Berresfords who packed us in like sardines. When the bus seemed full to overflowing with people standing in the aisles the conductor made room for even more by the simplest of technology. As the bus approached the stop the conductor waited until we were about to pass before pressing the bell. The driver, alert to his command, stood on the brakes bringing the bus to a halt, and as its momentum sent passengers hurtling forward, another eight passengers jumped aboard. The conductors were well known with their own likes and dislikes and they eased the boredom of the routine trip with wisecracks and nonsense. Each bus stop had its special name or pronunciation, starting with Avnoo, Lion, Sylum, Ched Heath, Crystal Palace, Marble Arch and Leek Dead Centre - as we passed the graveyard at Compton Church.

The one conductor who stood out was a man called Jacka Bill. Jack was the son of 'Cheat' Turner who for years toured the village with a horse and cart from which he sold an array of vegetables. It was said that Cheat had a special set of scales that enabled him to systematically rob every one of his loyal subjects. If Cheat was a one-off, it followed that Jack would be a true original. Christened John William after his father he was immediately re-christened Jacka Bill by the rest of the village and for the rest of his life he diligently adhered to his calling of rogue, rascal and layabout. We children adored him and secretly so did the rest of the village: except, as always, for one woman.

It all came about through Berresfords, of course. Jacka was in his element as a bus conductor with his ticket board and a leather bag full of money. This particular lady had spotted the bus approaching when she was some distance from the stop. Realising that she might miss it she began to run. Jacka spotted her and waited as she heaved her overweight and weary body aboard without a word of thanks. Flopping into her seat she glared at Jacka. "A return to Longton please" she said as she handed him a florin. "Longton?" said Jacka, "We aren't going to Longton missus!" "But it says Longton on the front" protested the lady. "Ee missus," said Jacka, "It says Persil on the back but we don't take in washing."

Hanley and Longton were about an hour away with Leek a mere twenty minutes and a fare of 3d return for children and 6d return for adults. The buses parked in the centre of town next to a thriving cattle market, and on a Wednesday we could wander among the stalls where sheep, cattle and horses waited to be sold. Perched high above the show ring the auctioneers spoke a quick fire language understood only by those in the know. With words flowing at the speed of light he would glance this way and that before a final dramatic pause when he would look hard towards a bidder, bring down the gavel and pointing to the new owner of a cow would say, "Your's Sir."

The farmers' wives meantime took advantage of their one day out as they joined the crowds that thronged a market square full of stalls, selling everything from clothes pegs to chamber pots. I walked among them all, looking nonchalant and turning over my pennies until the temptation to spend became to great. Then, with a flourish, my money would be gone. A young blood with money to spend had just hit town!

The farms themselves were only just beginning to modernise and the one along Station

Road showed no signs at all of coming to terms with the new agricultural era. If I did but realise it I was very privileged to spend some time with the Cope family at Muck Flood Farm. I never did know it as anything else. I just know that every year without fail the River Churnet overflowed its banks and flowed into the cow sheds and barns and occasionally into the house itself. Not that it made any difference to Bill Cope. Bill was the most laid back farmer of all time. Nothing worried him and he simply got on with his life without giving a damn for anyone or anything else. Something as insignificant as a flood would make no impression at all. All the local children visited the farm and helped with hay making, fed the animals or generally messed about around the cows, horses, ducks, fowl, dogs and cats that were part of farm life.

The best job of all was hay-raking. This was a pleasant job that even a small boy could do. A huge rake, supported by two large iron wheels and pulled by an amiable cart horse was used to draw the hay into long piles that spread across the field twenty feet apart. Sitting above the rake on a cast iron seat the driver simply pulled a handle to raise the tines and release the hay into the lengthening pile as the horse patiently ambled up and down the field.

The gathering of the hay, some of which was formed into a house shape rick, was hard work. The hay was tossed onto the rick or onto a cart by the use of a pitch fork. Throwing up the hay got harder and harder as the stack grew higher and higher. No respite was allowed as we all worked to get the field cleared before the weather broke and put everything back to square one. On a hot day, with our shirts off, and with hay seeds working their way past the belt on our trousers, we would end up with red backs and sore waists. The pictures painted by Constable and other country artists portray a false image; hay-making was hard work. In fact all the manual work on the farm was laborious, from potato picking to milking.

Milking especially was tiring to young hands but was clearly an essential part of dairy farming. The cows were quick enough to spot an amateur and wasted no time at all in

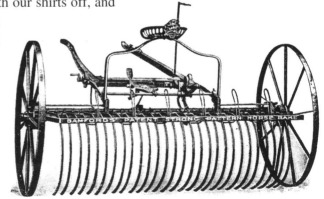

The pictures on this page are two adverts for Bamfords of Uttoxeter showing the haymakng equipment of my childhood.

raising a back leg and hooking me along with my bucket and stool into the broad channel that contained all the muck and pee. But a couple of kicks was enough to make even me learn to milk properly.

John Walter Winterton at Brook House Farm not far from us.

Farm animals in general seemed to be amazingly intelligent, non more so than the huge shire horses that were part of everyday life. They knew their way around the village milk rounds, stopping routinely outside each house while the milk was ladled into a jug or can. The Copes' horse, Bonney, had a great affinity with the farm hands and loved being fussed. After a days work, Bonney would head for the stables and stand patiently whilst her feed of hay was piled into place. Bonney's favourite trick was to gently place one of her hooves onto my foot as I stuffed the hay into the manger. As I tried to leave she would increase the pressure just enough to hold me. I knew the answer. I had to spend the next five minutes stroking her neck and talking to her until she decided she had had enough. Then, just as I was starting to panic she would raise her hoof and release me. She really was the most gentle creature.

Over the years I think we all spent time on Cope's farm. We were country children and pleased to be so. The weekly visits to Leek and the Cattle Market, our games and country pursuits were all we wanted from life. Leek was to become even more familiar when, at the age of eleven, I began my time at the Council School on Springfield Road. The school seemed huge in comparison to Cheddleton and poles apart as far as confidence and happiness were concerned. Academically I went from bad to worse and only began to improve when, at the age of sixteen, I attended the College of Further Education.

Leek County Secondary School for boys catered for the town's children plus all the boys from the surrounding villages. Warslow, Butterton, Onecote, Ipstones, Cheddleton and all the tiny hamlets in between sent their children by bus to Leek where the long suffering Stan Clowes, Trevor Harvey and an assortment of younger teachers tried valiantly to instill some discipline and knowledge into us. The curriculum was all very basic with arithmetic, science, English, history and geography competing for our time with woodwork, metalwork, gardening and physical training. In short we were being trained for manual work and Latin, Shakespeare and music were virtually ignored, as were O levels or School Certificates. Stan Clowes tried to give us an appreciation of music for a term before giving it up as a bad job. Strangely enough it is his lessons I remember so well and, from time to time, I find myself listening to Mozart and being transported back to school on the wings of a Magic Flute.

In the midst of the mayhem that passed for school life we also had the presence of the Poles. The Polish boys were the sons of the Polish soldiers and refugees who had been housed in the army camp at Blackshaw Moor after the War ended in 1946. In that remote and bleak camp the Polish families settled into a new life in a strange land and, as they struggled to make ends meet, they also struggled with a new language. Not only did those stoic families come to terms with this new life, they also integrated with the local community. The boys who attended Leek School had a tough time and on many occasion had to stand up for themselves both physically and mentally. Suffice to say they took everything life could throw at them and still came up smiling. I can honestly say that I never heard a Polish boy complain or grumble. If they had their disappointments they never showed it, neither did they express any regrets or criticise our alien culture. They were stoic to a man and contributed much to our school life.

Quite what social workers now would make of school discipline I dread to think. The teachers used a variety of methods to inflict punishment when deemed necessary and it was deemed necessary several times a day. Some teachers favoured a leather belt which was not too painful. Worse by far was the slipper, a shiny soled sandal which left an imprint of a red sole on your backside, or a sawn off cricket bat which left its mark for several hours. I must admit that, for the most part, the punishment was well deserved; who in their right mind would put detonator caps into the hinges of all the seats in the science lab, and how the devil did Trevor Harvey know who it was? For that little escapade I received six strokes of the Headmaster's cane, and decided enough was enough.

The only person on whom the punishment had no effect at all was my class mate, Barrie Mycock. Barrie originated from Staffordshire Moorlands and was a rebel from day one. He quickly grew into a six foot bean pole and from his lofty height looked down with disdain on the rest of us. Barrie was one of those bright lads who simply rejected anything that failed to take his fancy. His battle with authority continued throughout his school life - and from what I can gather long afterwards. His greatest claim to fame is to be found in the discipline book. Nine strokes of the slipper in one day and still undeterred. I think it was at that point the teachers gave up on Barrie.

I was to meet him again many years later and, to my delight, he was as obstinate as ever. His sense of humour was as obtuse as it had been at school. A few years ago Barrie's heart attack became due and for the sake of convenience it occurred as he was sinking a pint at a local pub. The usual panic set in followed by a brief assessment of his condition. An ambulance arrived in double quick time and Barrie was transported to the hospital cardiac ward where the prompt attention of the medical team saved his life. During the early hours of his recovery a cardiac specialist, on a routine visit, approached his bed. He examined Barrie thoroughly and then glanced down at his nicotine stained fingers. "Do you smoke Mr. Mycock?" "No" said Barrie. "Then how do you explain the nicotine on your fingers?" "It's from smoking." "But I thought you said you didn't smoke." "That's right. I packed up twenty minutes ago."

I think the doctors reached the same conclusion as the teachers. He made a full recovery which was only to be expected from someone who constantly bucks the system. The last time I heard from Barrie he was selling his farm consumables business and had an eye on retirement. That of course is the way we are all heading, or most of us, because some of those classmates of mine have already passed on.

Cheddleton 1953 Coronation Programme courtesy of R. Bold

Cheddleton Coronation Celebrations

In October 1952, a Public Meeting was convened by the Parish Council to form a Committee to organise the festivities in the Village in connection with the Coronation of Her Majesty Queen Elizabeth II.

The following Officers were elected :—

CHAIRMAN : Ald. H. Barber, J.P.
VICE-CHAIRMAN : Rev. J. H. Bowman
SECRETARY : Mr. J. H. Simcock
TREASURER : Mr. J. Barber

The following organisations in the Village have sent delegates to form the Committee :—

ASHCOMBE PARK C.C.
BADMINTON CLUB
BOWLING CLUB
BRITISH LEGION BRANCH
BRITISH LEGION BAND
CHAPEL
C. E. SCHOOL
EX-SERVICEMEN'S CLUB
GIRL GUIDES
LABOUR PARTY
PARISH COUNCIL
RED LION
ST. JOHN AMBULANCE
WOMEN'S INSTITUTE
J. BARBER & SONS, LTD.
BASFORD BRIDGE CARNIVAL COM.
BOY SCOUTS
BRITISH LEGION (WOMEN)
BRITTAINS' PAPER MILL LTD.
CHURCH
CONSERVATIVE ASSOCIATION
FREEHOLDERS
INFANT SCHOOL
MOTHERS' UNION
PLAYING FIELDS COMMITTEE
ST. EDWARD'S HOSPITAL
TENNIS CLUB
YOUTH FELLOWSHIP

Many of the above organisations have given very generous donations to help pay for the celebrations, and many individuals have given great help in preparing for the festivities.

A Festivities Sub-Committee was formed by the following :—

Mr. W. Bunn (Chairman), Mr. D. Nixon (Secretary), Misses Adams, Bold, Burndred, and Messrs. Boswell, Coghill, Rogers, and the Rev. J. E. T. Walters.

How CHEDDLETON will Celebrate the Coronation . . .

Coronation
JUNE 1953

Wednesday, 3rd June

Knock-Out Cricket Competition

FINAL

2ND INNINGS

ON THE ASHCOMBE PARK GROUND

beginning at 6-30 p.m.

PROGRAMME OF EVENTS

Monday, 1st June

Knock-Out Cricket Competition—FINAL

Previous matches have already been played between the following 8 teams:—

BLACK LION — RED LION

EX-SERVICEMEN'S CLUB — ST. EDWARD'S HOSP. 'A'

BRITTAINS, LTD. — ST. EDWARD'S HOSP. 'B'

BRITISH LEGION — CHURCH

THE FIRST INNINGS OF THE FINAL WILL BE PLAYED TO-NIGHT ON THE ST. EDWARD'S HOSPITAL GROUND, BEGINNING AT 6-30 p.m.

The Committee wishes to thank the Hospital and Ashcombe Park for generously lending their grounds, and also Mr. E. Lambert for arranging the Games.

Thursday, 4th June

OLD-AGE PENSIONERS' TEA
6-30 p.m. in the Churnet Hall.

Motorists will bring in old people who are infirm or who live a long distance away.

Catering by MELLOR'S of Lichfield; serving by ladies of the Village.

Entertainment by local artistes, including :—

Messrs. O. Eardley, J. Davidson and Kelso, R. Turner, I. Coghill, Mrs. F. Turner, and members of the Women's Institute.

CHEDDLETON — PAST AND PRESENT
A Village Survey

SESSION : Sept, 1953 — March, 1954.
THURSDAYS at 7-30 p.m.
(Ex-Servicemen's Club)

If you are interested in any aspect of Village life, you are invited to take part in this experiment. You may assist by becoming a member of the class, or by making available any special information, historical documents, books, maps, etc. which you possess.

TUTOR :— Miss H. E. S. Ainley-Walker, M.A., (N. Staffs. District, W.E.A.)

Full details from Mr. C. Spode, (Branch Secretary, W.E.A.) 4, St. Hilda's Avenue, Cheddleton.

Tuesday, 2nd June (Coronation Day)

1. A silver spoon, suitably inscribed, will be presented to any child born on this day.

2. Bottles of whisky (presented by Ald. H. Barber and Capt. W. D. Walker), will be presented to the oldest lady and gentleman resident in the parish for the last 25 years or more.

3. Two Television Sets will be installed in the Parish Institute for anyone to watch the Coronation Ceremony. See the "Radio Times" for time of showing. (The Committee wishes to thank the Institute Committee for lending the Hall free).

4. Three prizes will be offered for the best decorated House exterior and garden. Judging will begin to-day and will end on Friday evening.

The Judges are :—
Dr. and Mrs. J. H. Malloy
Mr. and Mrs. W. D. Walker

5. The Church will be floodlit to-night until midnight, and this will be repeated for each evening this week. (The Committee wishes to thank Britain's Ltd. for kindly lending the equipment).

6. Combined Religious Services will be held to-day as follows :—

8-30 a.m. Holy Communion. 6-30 p.m. Special Service

7. There will be a Grand Dance in St. Edward's Hospital to-night from 8 p.m.—1 a.m., to Tim Wray and His Band. Admission 1/6 by ticket only.

8. A bonfire will be lit on the Playing Fields to-night, organised by the Scouts under Mr. R. Coghill. This will link up with bonfires which are being lit all over the country by the Boy Scout Movement.

I can say with some certainty that my days at Leek Council School were not exactly a success and, except for no longer being able to watch April Stanley and her class playing netball at the adjacent girls school, I experienced only the briefest regrets when I reached the age of fifteen and left for pastures new. On that last weekend of my schooldays I sat on our garden wall and for the final time as a schoolboy I waited for the twelve o'clock factory buzzer. It was Saturday, and as everyone came out and rushed home, I looked forward to going to work and earning a wage of my own. As the workers all disappeared the road once again became deserted except for a lone figure who casually smiled at me as he cycled slowly past. Roger Coghill was singing as he made his way home.

I had little time to reflect on during that last year at school. Jobs were plentiful in an age that relied more on labour than technology. The obvious place to go was Brittains Ltd. the place where my grandparents had spent their working life and the place that was as familiar to me as my own home. 1953 had been an extraordinary period. Events locally and nationally filled the newspapers in what turned out to be Coronation year. The young Princess Elizabeth was on holiday when King George died suddenly, and she and Prince Philip made a hurried return to London. The funeral of the King was the first solemn occasion to make an impact on me and although we did not possess a television, the News Chronicle carried several pages of text and pictures. The funeral was, of course, followed by months of planning for the Coronation.

The 1950s were revolutionary days for the average family. As we slowly recovered from the War the shops began to sell electrical goods. First Goblin and then Parnell introduced a robust washing machine complete with agitator and an automatic mangle. A refrigerator and a vacuum cleaner soon followed and housewives scrimped and saved for these labour saving devices. It seemed but a short time ago that the MEB were erecting electric poles along Station Road to bring electricity into our homes and street lights onto our roads.

Now we had endless possibilities before us. We still had to listen to the wireless as our main source of entertainment, but a television was what we coveted most. When a T.V. set finally appeared we sat around it enthralled. The lights were switched off to enhance the definition of the picture and one of us was poised ready to leap up and adjust the set when the picture began to slip off the screen. We had buttons to twist that were marked with the appropriate instructions: Horizontal Hold, Vertical Hold, Brightness and Contrast. If they failed to achieve a reasonable picture we simply thumped the top of the console. This usually shook the valves into life and the black and white images re-appeared on the nine inch screen.

Although the Coronation was an event of major significance it was obvious that only a privileged few would be able to watch it on their own T.V. so the Parish Council decided to invite the whole village to the Institute. Here a huge T.V. set with a fourteen inch screen and pictures that did not flicker or disappear had been placed high above the audience at one end of the room. Young and old gathered that day in the village to witness, for the first time, a national event. I realised later that similar situations occurred throughout the land. What is now commonplace was then unique. It was all happening that year. Even Mount Everest, so long the pinnacle of mountaineering ambition, succumbed to a team led by John Hunt. Hunt, the expedition leader was British and an exceptional climber, but it was the New Zealander Edmund Hillary and a Nepalese sherpa called Tensing who planted the Union Jack on the peak. The newspapers were full of it. Everest, the Coronation, and sporting achievements filled the pages - and in the Leek Post and Times an advertisement proudly proclaimed that Skinner & Co. of Derby Street, Leek, were proud to continue the unrivaled service they had given through five previous reigns.

There was certainly plenty to do in those days. In the same edition of the Leek Post and Times the New Grand was advertising its latest blockbusters, 'Painting the Clouds with Sunshine' and 'The Lure of the Wilderness'. The Palace, not to be outdone also had a double feature, 'Les Miserables' and 'The Thing From Another World'. If that was not enough I could catch a train at Cheddleton Station and go to the Alton Towers Gardens. Even I could afford the entrance fee of 9d..

A chap by the name of Hubert Newton could afford a lot more as the Leek and Moorland Building Society announced assets of £23 million pounds. The money was in big demand for the houses that were being built in and around the village. The Grange Road estate was the first of many that was to change the face of the village forever. The small village of our parents and grandparents began to disappear as the demand for modern houses with up-to-date amenities grew and grew.

My own little world began to revolve around sport. Local football teams produced local heroes and I practised long and hard to join the village side. Port Vale and Stoke City were our dream venues, and even Leek Town whose exploits in the Manchester League attracted a great deal of attention. Competing in the same league were Manchester United A and Manchester City A and many a future star cut their footballing teeth at Leek including the likes of Duncan Edwards, later to lose his life in the Manchester United Munich air crash. Most local villages competed in the Leek and Moorland League and that year, and for several years afterwards, three teams dominated. Cellarhead who drew its players from Bucknall, Werrington, Kingsley and Cheddleton, and Ipstones and Warslow very much village teams who, although on the face of it had limited choice, produced teams of exceptional quality.

The 1953/54 season finished with Warslow as worthy champions and Cellarhead and Ipstones just a few points behind.

	P.	W.	L.	D.	F.	A.	Points
Warslow	30	28	2	0	174	27	56
Cellarhead	30	24	4	2	159	43	50
Ipstones	30	23	4	3	136	55	49

The quality of the Warslow side can be clearly seen in the goals for and against columns. A strong defence and a brilliant forward line produced an average of six goals per match. Warslow was never the easiest place to visit. The local support could be both vociferous and very biased. Playing on the wing was intimidating to say the least, and being the referee demanded great strength of character. One of the stories passed down from season to season involved a referee who made a few unfortunate decisions that went against the home side. For his pains he finished up in the village duck pond. Bias notwithstanding, Warslow were a superb side although they eventually folded up and withdrew from the league. Cellarhead, on the other hand, continued to go from strength to strength and dominated the Leek Moorland league throughout its existence.

Cheddleton did not have a team at all at the time although the St. Edward's Hospital team kept the flag flying. The village side that included the likes of Ray Farrell and Doug Spooner had been successful for many years and had come to the end of its life. It was not replaced until 1956 when a revived Cheddleton P. F. team was accepted into the league. It was this team that my old school friends and myself aspired to. We finally made it towards the end of the 1950s and by 1960 the team included many of the boys from Cheddleton School including one of the best goalkeepers the village had ever produced:

A. Hemmings

D. Regg   A. Harrison

G. Pegg   A. Gibson   R. Hall

C. Banks   S. Lovenbury   R. Price   M. Profit   L. Johnson

Cheddleton P. F. like its predecessors, had a relatively short life and was eventually replaced by Cheddleton United. United themselves experienced mixed fortunes and were eventually replaced a decade later by a youthful side supported by the Cheddleton Sports and Social Club. At long last the village had a team to be proud of as Cheddleton S. & S. C. defeated all before them.

The other side of our sporting life revolved around cricket and Ashcombe Park, and we greeted with delight the news that Peter Judge had been appointed as the 'professional' for 1953. Peter Judge had played for Middlesex and Glamorgan and was a welcome addition to an already strong Ashcombe side. Peter's fortune in the Senior B league was mixed and his form varied from match to match as he tried to come to terms with the wide variety of pitches used by the local sides. In one memorable match all the effort became worthwhile. On that sunny Saturday we sat around the edge of the ground anticipating the sort of match we had come to expect from Michelin C. C. The Michelin Tyre Co. in Stoke-On-Trent employed over 6,000 people and as such could virtually guarantee a percentage of sportsmen and women who were anxious to represent their employer. The strength of the Michelin team lay in their bowling although on occasions their batsmen were good enough to cause problems for anyone. Their opening bowlers, Thornhill and Lowe, had a fearsome reputation. Joe Lowe, on his day, could match the performances of his youth when he was the mainstay of Cheadle Cricket Club and as fast as anyone in the league.

Ashcombe, winning the toss, elected to bat and as Jack Pointon and Duel Turner strode to the wicket we were confident of a sound opening. How misguided we were. Duel, so long the dependable opener, chose that day for one of his rare failures and was caught by Brock off Lawrence for a duck. Jack, tied down by Lowe's speed had opened tentatively enough but quickly gained confidence when Peter Judge joined him. Peter could do no wrong that day as the runs flowed from his bat with a fluency that broke the heart of the Michelin attack. One by one the rest of the side succumbed. Pointon was caught off a Joe Lowe special after contributing a useful 22. Corden followed with eleven runs to his credit and Gordon Alcock, the flamboyant number five, managed just nine before being trapped leg-before by Thornhill.

Just as we were about to panic Stan Alcock strode to the wicket and took up his stance, middle and leg. Obviously, we Station Roaders knew the match was as good as won. We had, after all, trained Stan to a peak of perfection. Even so we were still a bit anxious as Stan settled in before snicking a couple of off-cuts to get off the mark. For an hour Ashcombe regained the initiative and Peter and Stan took control. Just as our confidence began to outbid common sense, disaster struck. Lowe, digging deep into his reserves, found that little bit of extra pace and removed Stan's wicket before he could offer a stroke. With Stan gone for 25 Peter battled on as the lower order batsmen came and went. Peter was eventually caught by Adams off Thornhill as the Ashcombe innings petered to a close.

With seven extras to add we were just short of the 200 on 198. This score was enough to beat most teams but no one was taking the Michelin for granted and as the players retired for tea the tension built up in anticipation. We need not have worried. Peter Judge was having a dream match. Where he left off with the bat he started with the ball. Let there be no doubt, the Michelin were a good side, but on that memorable day they came across a master of his craft. Over twenty six overs Judge took 6 wickets for 75 runs.

The only thing to get the better of Judge was time and it was time that rescued Michelin. The match ended with Michelin on 172 for 9. A draw for them and a moral victory for us. That day remains vivid enough but it took the Leek Post & Times to remind me of the scores.

Ashcombe C.C. (v. Michelin) June 11th. 1953

J. Pointon	c.	Latham	b.	Lowe	22
D. Turner	c.	Brock	b.	Lawrence	0
P. Judge	c.	Adams	b.	Thornhill	111
N. Corden	c.	Dale	b.	Wood	11
G. Alcock	lbw.		b.	Thornhill	9
S. Alcock			b.	Lowe	25
H. Profit	c.	Dale	b.	Thornhill	2
B. Pegg			b.	Lawrence	6
R. Mellor		run out			3
T. Alcock		not out			1
R. Martin	c.	Dale	b.	Thornhill	1
				Extras	7
				Total	198

Ashcombe had a number of professionals who have spiced the teams' performance. There was also a strong influx of home grown talent. David Pegg bowled consistently well over many years but even he could not repeat the performance he achieved during our time at Leek School. I wonder if David's eight wickets for one run still stands in the record books.

Another fine bowler was Roy Jackson who drew the crowds to Cheddleton for several seasons. Whether it be Obediah Brassington, David Pegg, Roy Jackson, the Alcocks of yesteryear or the more recent performances of Ross Salmon, Ashcombe retains a special place in the heart of local sport.

Some of the professionals stand out. Fred Taylor was an exceptional bowler who topped the averages on several occasions. Khurshid Ahmed, the ex Pakistani batsman, inspired with the bat and, when he was joined by Sonny Ramadin, our enthusiasm knew no bounds. Ramadin produced match winning performances week after week and the crowds flocked to see him in ever increasing numbers. Temporary stands were erected and fences moved to accommodate the crowds. Car parking became a nightmare as spectators parked on the road sides and walked the last mile or so to the ground.

With the ground overflowing we had to call upon our ingenuity to get in. Usually Frank Kent, on the gate, would turn a blind eye as we sneaked past but when Sonny was on song we had to resort to other means. Whether it meant climbing the huge elm in the adjacent field or sneaking into Wardle's estate and then crawling under the fence behind the side screens the result was the same. We saw every match.

A. Corden

Mrs Wardle with deer in Ashcombe Park in the early 1950s.

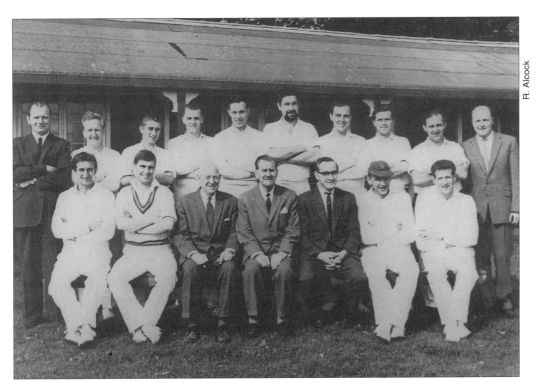

R. Alcock

Ashcombe Park C.C. Senior A champions 1966
Alan Pegg, V. Salmon, E. Sheldon, M. Sambrook, S. Wint, J. Hollinshead, J. Goodwin,
L. Beetham, F. Cooper, D. Holdcroft
R. Alcock, K. Morris, F. Glass, F. Bell, N. Corden, J. Shaw, G. Corbishley

Ashcombe Park C.C. Celebrations c 1960
A. Hazledine, P. Bailey, G. Deakin, F. Savin, W. Dishley, D. Turner, B Murrey
F. Glew, S. Ramadin, G. Alcock, F. Alcock, W. Conner

R. Alcock

Ashcombe Park C.C.
V.Salmon, F. Cooper, M. Proffit, M. Sambrook, J. Goodwin, G. Alcock,
S. Alcock, E. Sheldon, H. Proffit, J. Shaw, R. Alcock.

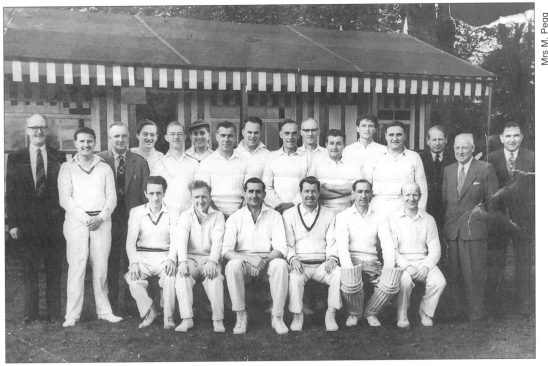

Mrs M. Pegg

Ashcombe Park C.C. 1960s
Tom Kent, C. Pegg, A. Hazledine, G. Alcock, F. Alcock, E. Sheldon, L. Hall, A. Mann, J. Alcock,
S. Alcock, D. Cartlidge, Roy Jackson, A. Brooks, W. Dishley, F. Glew, G. Thonger
Stan Alcock, V. Salmon, F. Taylor, J. Pointon, D. Turner, W. Flynn

A. Corden

An Ashcombe Park eleven early 1960s
W. Conner, D. Turner, S. Ramadin, P. Bayley, F. Cooper, R. Jackson, K. Ahmed, M. Sambrook,
J. Goodwin, G. Alcock, D. Hickman

Brittain's Knockout 1959 Machine Dept
G. Deakin, ? , ? , E. Steele, G. Pegg, S. Alcock, G. Alcock, D. Brassington
W. Conner, A. Lowe, D Pegg, ? , ? .

Brittain's Knockout 1959
N. Corden, J. Pointon, G. Pegg, H. Tidmarsh, G. Alcock, ? , ? . ? ,
E. Steele, A. Lowe, D. Pegg, ? , W. Conner, T. Conner.

Carnival Queen, Glenys Bateman, and her attendants.

Carnival Queen, Rosalie Shenton, attendants, and page boy Phil Cox.

Mrs R. Salmon

Carnival Queen, Rosalie Shenton, with Glenys Tatton and her attendants. Mrs Ada Shenton is at front left.

Glenys Bateman, Rosalie Shenton, and Joyce Shenton.

Attendants: Joan Toft, Jean Blakeman, ? McNicholl, Morag Clark, Sarah Clark, Margaret Jackson, Keith Goldstraw, Jean Conner, Hilda Beardmore, Gillian McNicholl, Dorothy Austin, Cath Rutter, ? Jackson.

Mrs R. Salmon

Carnival Committee about 1946.
J. Davidson, L. Clewes, ? , Mr Lowe, Mr Brassington, H. Weller
Mrs Cox, Mrs Spragg, Mrs Massey, Mr Bates, ? , Mrs Povey, Mrs Wetton, Mr Walker
Mrs Clewes, Mrs Weller, ? , Annie Goldstraw, Rosalie Shenton, ? , Mrs Walker, Mrs Shenton.

A. Corden

1st Cheddleton Scouts 1940s
L. Kent, K. Fielding, G. Griffiths
E. Glew, P. Mellor, A. Corden, E. Boswell, R. Clowes, D. Harrop.

PATRONS:

Messrs. Brittains Ltd.   Mr. J. Kirkland.
Messrs. F. Adams   Mr. F. Wetton.
Messrs. Garners   Mr. T. Alcock.
Misses J. R. Morton.   Mr. R. Day.
Messrs. Bourner, Bullock.   Mr. H. Lowe.
Mr. C. Durose   Mr. H. Sheldon
Mr. W. D. Walker.   Miss K. Lockett.
Mr. H. H. Weller.   Mrs. T. Cope
Mr. H. Barber.   Mr. H. Newton.
Mrs. C. Jackson.   Mrs Townsend.

Nurse Steel and Mrs. Clowes.

COMMITTEE:

Mr. Ward. Mr. W. Bell: Mesdames Wetton, Davison, Cox, T. Cope & W. Bell

OFFICERS:

President: Capt. W. D. Walker
Vice-President: H. H. Weller, Esq.
Chairman: Mr. T. Brassington
Hon. Treasurer: Mr. G. Carr
Hon. Secretary: Mr. J. G. Davison

SPECIAL MESSAGE TO SUBSCRIBERS

Ladies and Gentlemen.

It is my privilege, on behalf of the committee, to thank all those who so kindly help us in various ways for the causes for which we are working.

Since 1949 our efforts have been for Cancer Research and Local Blind, and we are proud to say through your help we have donated to those two causes over £2,000.

This is a grand achievement, so do please make July 23rd a date, and help us to have a successful day.

Yours sincerely.

J. G. DAVISON, Hon. Secretary.

268

BRITISH EMPIRE CANCER CAMPAIGN and LOCAL BLIND

Basford Bridge and Cheddleton

★

THE 17th ANNUAL

CARNIVAL FETE ★

Saturday, 23rd July, 1960

CROWNING
of
CARNIVAL QUEEN
(Miss C. L. Cope)

by

Mrs. C. Bode

OPENING CEREMONY
3 p.m.

by

C. F. BODE, Esq.

Programme 6d.

R. Bold

PROGRAMME

⁕

GRAND PARADE

Leaves "RED LION" at 2 p.m.

Parade Marshal:

MR. T. BRASSINGTON

⁕

FANCY DRESS

BEST ORIGINAL CHARACTER (Boy or Girl)	10/- 7/6
BEST COMIC CHARACTER (Boy or Girl)	10/- 7/6
BEST ORIGINAL CHARACTER (Lady or Gent)	£1 10/-
BEST COMIC CHARACTER (Lady or Gent)	£1 10/-

NO GROUPS ALLOWED

We are pleased to acknowledge the donations For Cancer Research kindly given in memory of their loved ones, by relatives.

⁕

Attractions on the Field

AT ASHCOMBE PARK

⁕

HANLEY PIPE BAND

CHEDDLETON EX-SERVICEMEN'S BAND

M A Y P O L E   D A N C I N G

B A B Y   S H O W

(Judged by Nurse Steele and Mrs. Clowes)

C H I L D R E N ' S   S P O R T S

F A N C Y   D R E S S

S I D E   S H O W S

G r a n d   P r i z e   D r a w

Lucky Programme Number

Licensed Bar on Field

Grand Carnival Dance

8 p.m. — 12 p.m.

C H U R N E T   H A L L

Dance 3s.   Regency Band

M.C.s: MR. and MRS. WARDLE

Public Address by Cadman's of Hanley

Brittain's 1932.

The laundry at St Edward's hospital.

Chapter Six
A Working Man

The thought of working for a living filled me with great excitement. Gone were my schooldays and the constant search for odd jobs to earn pocket money. Soon I would be a man of means. I polished my shoes, pressed my trousers and, with a freshly scrubbed face and brylcreamed hair, I set off to see the personnel manager at Brittains Paper Mills.

Dickie Shemilt peered over his glasses at me, "Whats your name?"

"Alan Gibson" I replied.

"Any relation to Bill Gibson?" he said. "

He's my grandfather."

He paused for a moment. Was this a good sign, or a bad one? I sat there, my conversation exhausted. The interview was not going well.

"What can I do for you then?"

Here was my big moment, the time to speak my well rehearsed lines.

"Have you any vacancies to offer me please ?"

He was obviously taken aback by my command of interviewing technique and felt compelled to offer me a job immediately. I was told to report on Monday, at 8.00am, to Mr George Oynton, the boss of the sorting shed. I was to be paid the sum of £2-10s a week. For the first few months it was agreed that my mother would keep £2 and I would have 10/- pocket money. One of the older men at the paper mills put me right on the subject of money. He suggested that control of my ten shillings was absolutely vital. "Take it from me lad - you should never spend more than 7s.6d per week on wine, women and song; that will always leave you half a crown to squander." Excellent advice for anyone. After the first months I paid board and lodgings of 25s. a week and kept the remaining 25s. for clothing and expenses.

Work in the sorting shed was a wonderful experience. The place was full of elderly women, all thirty plus! It was the job of Mrs Hazeldine, Mrs Owen and a dozen others, whose names I forget, to sort through piles of raw material and remove any bits of wood, rubber or metal. The material was then baled and taken into the paper mills for processing. It was the job of several boys to bring in truck loads of the hemp-like raw material to the women and to remove the same when it had been sorted. It is probably appropriate to say this was money for old rope! There were also mountains of a fluffy wool like substance that had to be sorted and the women would sit for hours chatting and laughing amongst themselves as this tedious job continued.

The monotony was broken only by the light programme on the radio which played all the latest songs. Every now and then the ladies would join in as a particular favourite came over the air. The sound of 'Save the Last Waltz for Me' filled the room. George Formby with his ukulele and Workers Playtime went down particularly well - especially as the compere always managed to put down the foreman of whichever factory they were visiting.

George Oynton ruled over us with a rod of rubber and, once we had got ahead of the ladies, we would spend hours larking about. It all seemed to be part of a tried and tested plan and before long each of the boys were transferred to a more permanent position. In my case it was the Tin Shed. The Tin Shed was in fact an old wooden building where George Dale, a long established bachelor, tried to control a group of youngsters and train them in the art of producing tin foil. The process involved the smelting of metal ingots which were then dissolved in hydrochloric acid. At a later stage a number of zinc sheets were added to the acid solution and the reaction, over 24 hours, produced a thick scum like paste. This paste, after much washing and filtering, was turned into a paint like fluid that was applied to the surface of tissue paper. The final act of calendering produced a bright shiny surface that was an excellent conductor of electricity.

The transition from schoolboy to worker was to transform me. My confidence was restored, as my ignorance was overshadowed by the inevitable ability of youth to think they know everything. I decided that education was important after all and looked around for ways of self improvement. I indulged myself by purchasing Winston Churchill's *A History of the English Speaking Peoples*. The day the book arrived and I handed over my first instalment remains with me to this day. I adored those four volumes that opened up the world to me.

My next purchase was in the form of a correspondence course from the Metropolitan College and my eager mind began to expand. It was essential that I changed my job and in those days it was considered vital for a working class lad to have a trade. In my case I desired to be a maintenance fitter. The problem was how. I decided on positive action and determined to put my request to the Engineering Director, Herbert Weller. Mr. Weller lived in one of the paper mill houses not far from our humble abode and, as I was in the Scouts and he was the County Commissioner for the Scout movement, I quickly found a way of speaking to him. Since an earlier confrontation had occurred when I burnt down his orchard, he listened to my plea with remarkable calm and promised to see what he could do.

He was as good as his word and shortly afterwards I was transferred to the engineering section where I was set to work in the boiler house and the fitting shop. It was not quite what I was expecting but it served well enough. Mr. Weller also suggested that I studied for a City and Guild certificate in engineering at Leek College of Further Education and later at Stoke Polytechnic. By now my confidence knew no bounds. I had a girlfriend, a trade and the chance to make amends for my failure at school.

My examination success continued unabated for some time and I was only brought down to earth by the arrival of a long brown envelope that bore the initials O.H.M.S. The contents informed me that I was to attend the Bethesda Street Clinic in Hanley for a medical examination. Apparently my Country needed me. National Service was in fact being phased out at the time and anyone serving an apprenticeship could claim exemption. So I had a golden opportunity to avoid conscription but, for some strange reason, I elected to attend.

As the day of the medical dawned I donned my best gabardine mac and took the Berresfords bus to Hanley. I walked nonchalantly down Piccadilly, up past the Theatre Royal and crossed the road to Bethesda Street. I entered the room marked 'Army Medicals' and found myself with about thirty others, mainly from the Potteries. They stood in groups and most of them seemed to know each other. It was obvious from their mutterings that they did not relish the thought of army life and I resisted mentioning that I had decided that the army would be a good way to spend two years and to see the world.

The mutterings of discontent came to an abrupt end with the arrival of a sergeant and a man in a white coat. We were told to form a line after which the sergeant quickly proceeded to check our names and tick his list. "Right lads. I now want you to get undressed. Hang your clothes over there and collect a sample bottle from the table by the toilet block".

Somewhat embarrassed we undressed and went to collect our bottles. "I require a urine sample off each of you", said the sergeant.

Now if you actually want a pee this is fine, but if you do not, you have a problem. The result was an infinite variety of urine samples. Some bottles contained a few spots of a miserly effort while others were full to the brim and dripping onto the floor.

We now stood in a row trying to look as natural as possible. Unable to hide our modesty because of the samples we were carrying we shuffled along hoping to god that we didn't have an erection or worrying that our private parts looked too small. We were ushered into an adjacent room where a row of cubicles awaited us. I entered one and found a medical orderly waiting for me. I was told to bend down while he looked up my backside. Quite what he expected to see I will never know! Having then examined my chest he came to the most delicate part of the examination. Reaching for his pencil he lifted my balls and said cough. I would like to be able record that I broke his pencil but I can make no such claim.

I was told to get dressed and go into yet another room. Here the man in the white coat sat at a desk at the far end of the room. I was told to stand about twelve feet away and face the right hand wall. In a low voice he asked me the date and the time and after I had replied I was instructed to face the other wall. I did so and waited for the next question. It never came, or at least I never heard it. He raised his voice and asked me to come to the desk where he shone a small light into my right ear. "Do you realise you have a perforated ear drum?" he said. "Yes" I said "but I think I can hear O.K."

He was obviously not impressed and told me I had failed the medical. I left the room with a green card and a heavy heart! As I walked towards the exit some of the less enthusiastic conscripts looked at the green card in my hand. I could swear I heard them muttering something to the effect of jammy bastard.

For the time being my destiny would remain at Brittains Paper Mills and my time there was as happy as it was uneventful. But in the course of time marriage and children were to concentrate my mind on matters of finance and ambition. I had a need for both and the temptation of greater earnings and greener grass would lead me to pastures new.

I worked for some years as a maintenance fitter with the Michelin Tyre Co and also with the Electricity Board at Meaford Power Staion. As much as I enjoyed the work I could not foresee a long term career for myself as a fitter. I wanted more and to obtain more I needed to progress into management. This was the hardest step to make. Stereotyped ideas and a reluctance among employers to transfer someone from the shop floor to the office had to be overcome first, but after a few false starts I managed it. I joined JCB as a buyer and then moved to Croxden Gravel Co. as a manager. Not that I earned much more but at least I had made a start on the ladder.

It was at this point that my feet began to itch again. I knew my way around by now, I was confident and progressing well enough, but in my mind there was growing need to expand my horizons. My dream was to go to New Zealand - whether permanently or for a few years did not really matter. As much as I loved Cheddleton , the thought of remaining rooted in one place all of my life appalled me. I had to see some of the world. I needed to experience other cultures and peoples.

Vera, with the patience of Job, had long since accepted my wanderlust, but even she was somewhat taken aback when I suggested we sell up and take our chances in New Zealand. With some trepidation she agreed. This was 1971. Our house went on the market and sold surprisingly quickly for the princely sum then of £7,500. In the meantime I was busy writing to companies in Christchurch in the hope of finding a job.

What few qualifications I had did not seem to impress anyone, but just as my spirits began to sink I received a telex from a man called Aubrey Smith. Aubrey, an Englishman, was the sales manager for an agricultural machinery company there. Not only could he offer me a job of sorts, he could fix us up with temporary accommodation. This was a wonderful stroke of luck and a gesture of generosity I subsequently learned was typical of New Zealand people.

Now we were all set. We disposed of most of our belongings except our Vauxhall Viva which we shipped out to our new home near Christchurch. All our capital was transferred to Lloyds New Zealand amd we prepared for our first ever plane journey. The trip took 28 hours with only the briefest of fuel stops for refuelling. Such an exhausting flight affected us all. It was a big mistake and one we have avoided ever since.

We arrived in New Zealand jet-lagged and shattered. To his eternal credit, Aubrey was there to meet us as we dragged ourselves apprehensively into the arrivals lounge at Christchurch Airport. The accommodation he had found for us was in a small hotel called the Peoples' Palace. It turned out to be an organisation run by the Salvation Army, but it was clean and comfortable and cheap enough while we looked for a house to rent. These were plentiful enough and within a few days we were ensconced in an old clapboard house in a leafy suburb called Shirley, just a few minutes away from Andrews and Beaven, my new employers.

Within no time at all Susan aged 8 was settling into school, Mark had a job as an apprentice chef, and although Vera, like me, had to drop down a peg, she was able to find part time work in a nursing home. My aspirations in truth suffered a blow when I arrived for work that first morning at Andrews and Beavan. The only job available was as an assistant in the engineering stores, and then I was unfamiliar with agricultural components and with the systems they were operating. But they were not going to change for me. It was obvious that I would have to lump it and fit in with new disciplines and procedures. I was well and truly at the bottom of the ladder and the only way up had to be up. Gradually I became a little more useful and less of a liability, and Aubrey continued to give me his support. Aubrey and his wife became our close friends and slowly guided us into New Zealand life.

We had been in Christchurch for about six months when we decided to take the plung and buy a bungalow - or 'single storey' as the locals call them. The property was all we had dreamed of although it was modest enough, and the risk was worth taking as I had by now a better job lined up. the outlook was looking very rosy.

I landed a job as store manager with Atlas Cookers, New Zealand's largest appliance manufacturers. My salary doubled and over a very few years it continued to rise as I was promoted through various management posts. We were now earning three times the national average and living the New Zealand dream; with blue skies and sunshine, endless beaches, snow-capped mountains, inland lakes, New Zealand is idyllic.

But despite all this we suffered periods of nostalgia for England. Home sickness clouded our dream. Our two children were growing up quickly. What if they settled totally to New Zealand - how could we then return to England if we wanted? Vera loved Christchurch but wasn't sure she wanted to stay there permanently, and my own feelings were much the same. We had to make a decision soon. In retrospect now - and that is always very easy - I think I got it wrong. We made the decision to return to the UK and we decided to be very positive about it. We could after all return again within two years couldn't we - England could be classed as a holiday.

Once again we put our house on the market, and once again it sold very quickly. It fetched twice what we had paid for it and with an excellent exchange rate at the time we returned with an excellent financial footing in the the UK.

But even the best laid plans in life get altered. Within weeks of arriving back I was offered a job at JCB at a salary I couldn't refuse. I took it and with it I sealed our fate. I am sure at the time Vera and the children would have gladly returned quite quickly to New Zealand, but with such a good job we could enjoy our life in England and afford to return to Christchurch from time to time for holidays.

The biggest shock I had on our return to England was to discover that Brittains Paper Mills were in a state of terminal decline. How and why was to puzzle me for years to come.

New Zealand. Kaikoura Mountains, north of Christchurch.

Brittain's 1922.

Chapter Seven
Brittains Paper Mills

The history of paper making in Cheddleton is so well documented elsewhere as to make a detailed history here repetitive but a brief summary is relevant to what follows. The influence of Brittains Paper Mills on the people of Cheddleton village has been immense. From 1797 when William Adams purchased mandow from the Rev. Edward Powys with the intent of producing hand made paper for the pottery industry, it offered employment to the village.

With first the introduction of canals and then the railway it became both practicable and economic to transport the paper from the Churnet Valley to the towns and cities of England. By the mid 1800s the Churnet Valley Railway and the Caldon Canal were in full competition.

Paper making advanced and improved technology brought to the works by the Fourdrinier dynasty increased the volumes and quality. The paper mills of Cheddleton, passed through the hands of a variety of owners, grew to meet an increasing demand. Familiar names in the village began to appear: William Goldstraw, Jeremiah Steele, Thomas Brittain and Frederick Hough. By the late 1800s the mills, now bearing the name Brittains Ltd, covered several acres. The original Butchers Meadow, long since swallowed up by industrial growth, was now an appendix to the paternal factory that supported the whole village.

Cheddleton was a lucky village. Guaranteed employment was the accepted norm. What the historian omits, because such facts are intangible, is the benevolence and integrity of Brittains Paper Mills. Such attributes are not achieved by overnight success or the get rich quick attitude of the opportunist. The whole ethos of Brittains was nurtured over two centuries by men of integrity and sound business acumen. Generation after generation of Cheddleton men and women relied upon the paper mills for their livelihoods. Such was the security of employment and reliability of the management in making sound profits, employees were confident to take the normal risks of life. Local financial institutions, banks and building societies were happy to arrange loans and mortgages for employees of Brittains, secure in the knowledge that Brittains looked after its employees and repayments were unlikely to be reneged on. The philosophy of the company was simply enough. Quality first, regardless of everything else, had been the basis of its success, and Brittains, the Steels and the Haighs, stuck rigidly to this winning formula.

The art of paper making reaches a peak in the production of fine tissue. This skill is not something to be learned at college or taken from a text book. As much as anything it is a case of practice makes perfect and, although Brittains had all the scientific equipment and qualifications to support the latest technology, it also had the lifetimes of experience of its papermakers. Staff who spent up to fifty years producing a quality product developed an instinct that told them when that precise mix of water and fibres was perfect or if the machines needed to go faster or slower, or the temperature and drying required a nip here or a tuck there. The quality systems were in place and rigidly adhered to but it was the inherent skills of the Cheddleton paper makers who made such testing a formality - and guaranteed the high quality Brittains was world famous for.

It is fair to say that workers wishing to earn more money could do so in the towns of Stoke-on-Trent, the JCB factory at Rocester or at GEC in Stafford for instance. Brittains paid

Panoramic view of Brittains about 192?

wages on a par with other industries in the area which in essence is precisely what any shrewd employer would do. What it also did, far better than anyone else, was to look after its workforce. A personal interest by the directors in local affairs gave them a sound insight into the problems of families, and when help was required, help was given.

They knew more about the youngsters who joined the company than the youngsters themselves. Family background, personality traits, determination and ambition were all part of the person they looked for when they were employed. Virtually every youngster was given time to acclimatise, pranks and escapades were overlooked, and football, cricket, scouts and guides actively encouraged, as was membership of the Company's Fire Brigade and St. John Ambulance. There was even a small chapel within the factory for those whose needs were more spiritual. It was this attitude of benevolence and integrity, plus the job security, that made up to one thousand employees content to spend much or all of their working lives in the employ of Brittains Paper Mills. It was not uncommon for a man to spend fifty years within the confines of that one, ever growing company.

As the company grew so did its reputation. The name of Brittains was synonymous with quality the world over. The management of Brittains would no doubt be described as fastidious but staid - the directors were schooled by their predecessors in the art of steady progress, low risks and positive profits, a tried and tested system of management which resulted in a cash rich and debt free company that could progress at its own speed, and maintain its interest in technology and its reputation for quality. In the years leading up to the 1960s a cheque from Brittains Paper Ltd was as good as a bankers draft.

With the advent of the 1960s there came the financial pressures needed to modernise machinery which, in some cases was over fifty years old. Britain had rested on its laurels after the War and now the international competition from more modern economies was beginning to bite. Attempts were made to finance the expansion and the building of new mills through Company funds and directors' personal financial input. Sidney Hill found it necessary to secure an overdraft facility of £1,000,000 for the Company. In 1963 the responsibility for financial control lay with a board that will be familiar to those who know the old Brittains:

Sidney Hill.   Chairman   John Charles Holmes.
John Phillips Scarratt.   Managing Director.   Kenneth Roy Latchford.
Nicholas Howard.   George Harry Norman Pickford.
John Frederick Haigh.   M. F. McDonnell. F. C. I. S.   Company Secretary.

The Engineering Director, Mr. H.H. Weller, retired at the end of 1963.

The Company accounts were not obliged to divulge sales turnover but there was a trading profit of £563,003 (against £482,844 for 1962) before depreciation and taxation, giving a net profit of £234,059. To compare the figure with 1999 values a multiple of about 30 must be used (a semi detached house in Cheddleton cost about £2,000 in 1960 and about £60,000 in 1999). Conservatively a multiple of 25 would give a net profit of £5,751,475.

Although salaries were relatively low even at directors level, the payment of dividends was always generous. On this occasion it was no less than 24%, indicating a degree of largesse which would seem questionable by today's standards.

Prior to the 1960s and the huge overdraft, the reserves in 1959 reveal liquidity at £424,000. To appreciate the significance of this figure multiply at least by 25 again.

Whatever comments may be expressed about the directors of Brittains Paper Mills; staid, parochial, cautious or anything else, they were successful enough in the 1950s. A company trading in 1999 with liquid assets of £25,000,000 would be much admired, which is precisely the way the world viewed the Brittains Paper Mills of the 1950s. In retrospect the decision to become a Public Limited Company may not have been the wisest move, although it was made with the best of intentions. The ever increasing costs of technology and the need to increase sales world-wide was considered beyond the financial capabilities of the existing company. By converting to a public company and by the issuing of millions of shares an influx of cash was virtually guaranteed. Whether the board lost a little confidence in themselves or whether the financial institutions who took up the shares applied pressure is difficult to ascertain, but it was deemed essential to add financial experience to an already successful team of directors.

An influx of new directors gave the board a greater mix of experience. Sandy Wright had an in depth knowledge of general paper making and the later additions of Scott and Rickless introduced expertise in plastics and finance. The board of 1964 shows the last of the old names plus the addition of Mr. J.E.Rowe. Mr. Rowe had previously been with the troubled B.S.A. group who at that time were fighting for survival.

Board of Directors 1964.

S. Hill	Chairman.	J.C. Holmes
J.P. Scarratt	Managing Director.	K.R. Lachford MBE
N. Howard		G.H.N. Pickford
J.J. Haigh B.A.		J.E. Rowe F.C.A.

By 1967 Phil Scarratt was coming to the end of a long and distinguished career and, although he remained on the board for some time afterwards, he relinquished his position of

St John's Ambulance Brigade, Brittain's Ltd, 1950s.

St Johns Ambulance Brigade. Brittain's Cheddleton Division 1928.

THOMAS BRITTAIN.
Born 26th October, 1803.
Died 25th October, 1894.

THOMAS BRITTAIN, JUNIOR.
Born 12th February, 1838.
Died 31st January, 1885.

JOSEPH CECIL CLAY.
Born 24th March, 1847.
Died 21st September, 1924.

FREDERICK HAIGH.
Born 24th February, 1853.

Directors of Brittain's Paper Mills

A flooded Churnet alongside Brittain's paper mills.

Brittain's Volunteer Fire Brigade 1948

J. Pearson, P. Shenton, K. Kent, W. Tait, G. Kirkham

G. Corden, F. Pickering, E. Clowes, W. Sheldon, S. Oxford, R. Coghill, T. Alcock, A. Burdred, A. Hazledine, R. Austin, L. Walters

P.R.Mellor, W. Whittingham, R. Shemilt, M.I. Jackson, W. Burndred, L. Sutton.

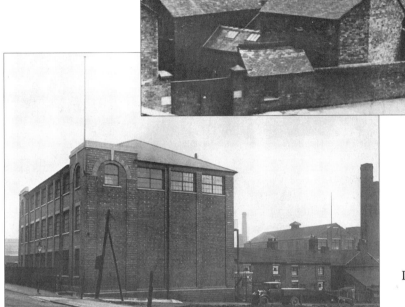

Brittain's Ltd
Ivy House Hanley
Mills 1908.

Below:
Directors of Brittain's
Paper Mills 1932.

Frank S. Bell.

Ernest F. Latchford.

Alfred Haigh.

Joseph H. Hill.

Benjamin J. Bell.

H. J. F. Ward.

managing director. In 1966 Mr. Stuart Mallinson was appointed to the board as finance director. Profit after taxation was down slightly for the year, but nevertheless showed a very healthy £317,121. 1968 saw the introduction of Mr J.C. Holmes as joint managing director along with Mr. K.R. Latchford and, more significantly, the retirement of J.E. Rowe and Sidney Hill. In two short years Brittains had lost the services of two of its shrewdest directors, with the demise of Hill and Scarratt.

At this point it is worth considering the way the company operated under the control of Sidney Hill and Phil Scarratt. Following a long tradition the company traded in paper and coated papers for;

> The electrical industry :
> Electrolytic capacitor tissues
> Lacquer coated interleaving capacitor tissues
> Kraft coil winding papers
> Tin coated capacitor tissues
> Insulating paper
> Metallised film
> Carbon paper manufacture.
> All rag, part rag and all wood carbonising.
> Tissues for typewriter and pencil carbons.
> All rag tissue for typewriter ribbons.
> Heliograph and Billing carbon base papers.
> Thermographic tissues.
> Manufacture of decalcomanias.
> Flat duplex.
> Flat Masterdecal and Thermaflat.
> Flat Simplex.
> Flat collodcon coated.
> Prestacel and release paper for dry strip decalcomanias.
> Self adhesive papers.
> Pottery and glass industry.
> Pottery printing tissue.
> Glass transfer tissues.
> Others.
> India paper - mainly for bibles.
> Airmail paper.
> Gauze stereotyping paper.
> Cigarette paper.
> Skin transfer tissue.
> Stencil paper for screen process printing (stenplex).

All these products were sold worldwide.

Towards the end of the 1960s with Sidney Hill suffering a heart attack and Phil Scarratt's retirement, the company continued a course that had been set over the decades. The old machinery and a failure to invest adequately in new technology now proved to be the stumbling block.

In the first of many changes Brittains-Riegel Industrial Products, a joint venture with an American company, was formed and a plant was built at Wrexham to accommodate the move into industrial laminates. It is thought that the Wrexham factory cost £100,000.

The 1970s heralded an unbelievable spate of acquisitions as the board sought to diversify and thus reduce its dependency on paper making. During the 1960s and 1970s diversification was certainly the name of the business game. Those who succeeded with the strategy did so because the need for a close understanding of the various businesses was recognised. Close monitoring and a multi-disciplined acumen were vital to the success of diversification. It was also vital to have adequate finance during the early years of a take-over to allow for managerial and technological changes while the new acquisition adjusted to group demands.

Acquisitions. Brittains Group.

1968	Brittains-Riegal Industrial Products
1970	Towgood & Beckwith - Became Brittains Arborfield
1970	W H K Products Ltd
	Macclesfield Engineering - part of WHK 1974
	Fanflow - part of WHK
	Hallam Engineering - part of WHK
1970	G. H. Piggott & Son - Became Brittains Plastics 1973
1970	Bradbury Bros. Ltd - Became Brittains Paper & Packaging Ltd.
1972	Brittains Wildblood Ltd. (Paper)
	Allan B. Carlisle & Sons (Converters)
	J. Downey (Sacks) Ltd. (Plastics)
	Kenmac Construction Co. Ltd.
	Wilde Civil Engineers later Brittains Tunnelling - part of Kenmac
	Summerton Design - part of Kenmac
	Brittains Plant - part of Kenmac
	Kenneth Johnson Ltd. - part of Kenmac
	Strataboard
1973	Brittains Building Supplies - part of Kenmac
	G. Priestner Ltd (Haulage)
1975	D. E. Haywood - Ins.Broker - became Brittains Ins. Brokers Ltd.
	Cityscope Investment - part of Brittains Ins. Brokers Ltd.
	Brittains Hospital Supplies Ltd.
1977	Wolvercote Paper Mills - formally Oxford University Press

Other names involved:

Brittains World Freight, formed by Brittains Ltd. 1975, transport office.
Brittains Paper Japan, formed by Brittains Ltd. 1975, selling office.
Holtschoppen & Brittains GMBH.   1972, German sales office.
Humphrey Reid & K.C.Plastics, part of Manchester sales office.
Brittains (Australasia) PTY Ltd. 1969, selling office.

Many of the companies mentioned were in fact formed by Brittains itself either to improve efficiency or to retain costs within the group, with considerable sums of money being saved by the insurance company and by the freight company.

By 1972 a reduced board of directors indicates the growing influence of Mr. S. Mallinson who became Managing Director in that year.

K.R. Latchford MBE	Chairman	J.F. Haigh
J.C. Holmes	Deputy Chairman	G.H.N. Pickford
S. Mallinson	Managing Director	

Not everyone was happy with the changes in the boardroom, or the pressures being exerted by a restless workforce. In the works the unions demand for wage increases continued unabated. Whilst the workers demand for more money reached breaking point the directors continued to purchase other companies. With morale at an all time low the Transport and General Workers Union was called upon for support. A short and acrimonious strike brought the dispute to an end and an increase in pay. The problems of employee relations led to the employment of Bill Forbes, an expert in trade union practises as a replacement for John Haigh in the personnel department. Forbes became a vital cog in the negotiations between the workforce and the management although his advice was not always followed. The following memo was obviously not welcomed by Forbes who had expressed his opposition for the suggestions therein:

FUTURE PERSONNEL POLICY.
To;- S.M./L.C.W./I.T./W.E.F.   From;- Mr. T.A.K. Wright.
Notes on Meeting held in the Boardroom at 11 a.m. on Monday, 1st July, 1974

In welcoming Mr Ian Torevell the Chairman said that the purpose of his appointment is to strengthen the Personnel Department in order that the Company can carry out a major rethink of its policies towards its employees in all grades. Our objectives can be summarised as follows :

To devise and execute a programme of reforming attitudes and employment conditions in order to eliminate the feeling of "us and them" between staff and workpeople and to substitute a unified approach across the board to individual rewards and benefits based on skill and responsibility and regardless of the nature of the job.

The Chairman then reminded the Meeting that three aspects had already been discussed but that so far no satisfactory answers had been arrived at. These are ;
a) a general sick pay scheme which would pay a basic weeks wages during a period of sickness
b) free transport to and from work in buses in line with the scheme already in existence for staff and
c) abolition of the practice of "clocking in"

Discussion centred round a further problem which is basic to any progress. This is that while the general levels of take-home pay probably compare well in the locality, this is only achieved by people working long hours at lower than average hourly rates. Considerable discussion has taken place on many occasions in the past regarding so called "productivity deals" as a means of solving this problem, so far without producing any answers. The general feeling is that there is little scope in this Company for a traditional type of productivity deal, which would produce a share out of more cash for the employees and additional profits for the Company. It is more likely that what we should be aiming for is a situation where working hours can be reduced while take-home pay can be maintained without any increase in the total labour force, thus producing a break even situation for both the employee and the Company. One point of view put forward was that if it is the Company's policy to reach a "productivity agreement" of this sort then all the various fringe items mentioned above and others be included in the negotiating package rather than be put in effect without strings.

The general feeling of the meeting was that a productivity deal about manning levels, hourly rates, take-home pay and methods of payment is not really concerned with fringe benefits. Furthermore, the majority of those present were prepared to view the removal of certain social inequities some of which, such as sick pay schemes and better pension provisions would add to costs, on the basis of the general good which would arise from the improvement of employer/employee relations if not on the basis of the financial return to the Company. It was felt that by creating this better environment the chances of avoiding trouble in the future and negotiating a better productivity deal would be vastly improved.

It was therefore felt that there is everything to gain by Management taking the initiative and treating as top priority the institution of a sick pay scheme, free buses and giving detailed consideration to the pros and cons of abolishing clock cards. It was agreed that the target date for completion of this phase should be December 1974. The Personnel Department will, therefore, immediately put in hand the necessary studies, costings and consultations with other companies who have taken similar steps. It is likely that implementation will require the education and changing of management attitudes and a programme for this will also have to be devised.

The various ways of replying to Mr Young's request for a meeting with the Directors to discuss a productivity deal were also discussed at some length. Various alternatives for the type and location of a meeting with him were discussed and it was agreed that these would be further considered and a recommendation made to the next Meeting.

Date of next meeting to receive progress report, Tuesday, 9th July at 3.30 p.m.

Despite Forbes opposition the proposed changes did in fact take place. Over a very short life the scheme cost the company a great deal of money before being disbanded in April 1975. Obviously Forbes was astute enough to recognise the potential problems and the opportunities for workers to abuse the system. It is equally obvious that he should have been listened to but the problems that ensued can hardly be blamed on the board of directors. It was a generous offer and a considerate effort to give the workforce improved conditions and equal status with office staff. Its abuse and subsequent failure must have been a great disappointment.

In the boardroom John Haigh resigned in June 1974. At subsequent A.G.M.s the Haighs, using their sizeable shareholding as a lever, attempted to get back onto the board but were unsuccessful. John Haigh's departure brought to an end an association with Brittains Ltd. that went back to its foundation. Dr Noel Strachen, a director of one of the group companies, also felt it necessary to resign and left the company shortly afterwards to take up a position with a Scottish paper company. The board of directors was beginning to look totally different to the familiar faces of the past. Directors. Group Board:

1975

K.R. Latchford MBE	Chairman
J.C. Holmes	Deputy Chairman
S.Mallinson FCA	Managing Director
J.C. Murphey BE	Founder director of Kenmac
P.R. Scott	Founder director Brittains Plastics
T.A.K. Wright	

1976

K. R. Latchford MBE	Chairman
S. Mallinson FCA	Deputy Chairman and Managing Director
V. Rickless FCA	
P. R. Scott	
T. A. K. Wright	

1977

K. R. Latchford MBE	Chairman
S. Mallinson FCA FCMA	Deputy Chairman and Managing Director
J. M. Jackson MA	At the behest of E.C.I.
D. J. M. Mitchell MA	At the behest of E.C.I.
V. Rickless FCA	
P. R. Scott	
T. A. K. Wright BA	

The board of 1977 was nothing like as harmonious as the board of 1973. The directors of Brittains most profitable years must have been well pleased with the profits of £1,189,044 in 1973 and £2,188,693 in 1974. The board showed all the signs of a good team heading for a rosy future; an opportunistic management giving full support to plans that would bring added prosperity.

The real problems came to a head in the latter part of the decade when the need to update machinery, advances in technology and world trading conditions put the company under immense financial pressure. The performance of some of the group companies was also being affected by difficult trading conditions and, as a result, a dramatic drop in profits in 1975 and 1976 was recorded. It should be recognised that despite the fluctuations in performance Brittains Ltd. never recorded a loss during the tenure of Stuart Mallinson.

It must also be recognised that changes in attitude, staffing levels and technological advancement would inevitably have led to redundancies. A classic example was quoted by one observer who noted how the company's wages department consisted of an office full of girls working on comptometers. In the same office a row of Borroughs Accounting Machines stood unprogrammed and unused. Can anyone really blame Stuart Mallinson for calling in the Burroughs engineers and having the machines programmed and put into use? That single action and the use of modern technology in the other offices resulted in thirty redundancies.

Throughout the final years redundancies at all levels were a recurring feature. The emotions attached to job loss and the difficulties of finding alternative employment resulted in the understandably biased views of the victims. It is a sad fact that redundancies should only be inflicted upon others. It is the job of directors and senior managers to anticipate trends and act accordingly. Despite the trail of despair leading from Brittains Ltd, the effects could have been far greater if timely redundancies had not taken place. Those who suffered will always blame the directors and point to their failings. Those who remained, and agreed that change was essential, will see Stuart Mallinson as the messenger rather than the cause. Most people agree that change was inevitable. Carrying out the changes was never going to place the managing director at the top of the popularity charts. Whether Mr. Mallinson and his fellow directors could have adopted a softer approach, or taken less drastic measures, will always be a question of debate, and a debate clouded with bias. There is certainly a case to be made in favour of those who point to periods of confusion. Headlines in The Sentinel did little to appease those who wondered what on earth was going on:

5TH AUGUST 1970:	**EXPANSION PLANS WELL ADVANCED**
18TH MARCH 1971:	**NO CHEDDLETON EXPANSION**
17TH APRIL 1975:	**OUR BIG YEAR** **CHEDDLETON FIRM CHIEF** **ANOTHER RECORD YEAR**
13TH MAY 1975:	**BRITTAINS HIT BY TRADING DOWNTURN**
1977:	**INCREASE OF 40 % IN TRADING PROFIT**
27TH JANUARY 1978:	**PAPER FIRM IN MAJOR EXPANSION**
1979:	**RECEIVER CALLED IN**

Business records of the 1970s point to periods of volatile trading on a global scale. Brittains in particular suffered from the loss of trade to Red China for no other reason than the countries decision to invest in inward technology and produce most of its own paper. In a document produced by Stuart Mallinson dated 31st June 1978 an assessment is made of the future profitability of Brittains Paper Ltd. The document also gives details of the company's background and goes into some detail about future expansion, sales potential, machine modification costs and the financial restructuring required to meet the demands of the 1980s. The document is extremely positive and is indicative of the optimistic mood of the directors. No thought of further redundancies or the possibility of bankruptcy emerges. The plans included a move to produce Simplex Decal Paper instead of purchasing the product from Tullis Russell. Consideration is also given to the transfer of the Hanley plant to Cheddleton, thus saving on transport and overheads. By producing Simplex Decal at Cheddleton an anticipated increase of 1,000 tons per annum would increase profits during 1979.

Marketing opportunities were re-established in Sweden, Yugoslavia, Spain, Italy, Mexico, America, Far East, Brazil, India, Europe, Australia and New Zealand. America especially offered unlimited potential and in many of the countries mentioned old contacts had been re-established and increased tonnage promised. The volume of future trade looked rosy indeed but depended very much on the upgrading of several of the older paper machines and the modification of No.13 and No.14 machines. The costs involved would run into several million pounds and the practicality of manufacturing would involve fewer machines and a twenty four hour production schedule involving four shifts.

In product terms many of the old favourites would continue to dominate the market and, to compete at world levels, the modified machines would increase volumes by 200 %. In addition consideration is given to a variety of new lines such as Laminating Tissue, Dog food bags, Lightweight food wraps, Tracing paper, Palachette papers (security printing), Etching papers, Glassine and Banknote paper. To meet the financial requirements negotiations had been successfully concluded with business financiers E.C.I. and with the added income from the sale of Brittains-Reigel at the beginning of 1978, the future of the company looked secure.

What followed was nothing short of farcical!

Date	Turnover	Net Profit	Overdraft	Remarks
1959	Not given	£315,065		Public Co. formed
1960	" "	£360,039		
1961	" "	£282,204		
1962	" "	£199,783		
1963	" "	£234,059		
1964	" "	£318,426		
1965	" "	£458,101		
1966	" "	£325,125	£295,744	
1967	" "	£317,121	£377,121	
1968	£4,001,897	£366,655	£775,411	
1969	£5,122,646	£508,024	£78,075	
1970	£6,759,449	£321,459	£801,367	
1971	£9,450,404	£292,189	£104,257	
1972	£12,398,143	£453,770	£212,319	
1973	£18,666,487	£1,189,044	£563,495	
1974	£24,651,065	£2,188,693	£382,159	
1975	£23,101,223	£748,727	£637,913	
1976	£27,244,320	£328,940	£846,308 (299,684)	
1977	£29,441,000	£600,706	£1,185,734	
1978	Loss anticipated			
1979	Return to profit anticipated			Receivers appointed.
1980	Modernised machines expected to increase world wide sales and seven figure profits.			

To appreciate the significance of outside influences during 1978, 1979 and 1980, an examination of documents produced at the time has to be considered. The contents of these documents illustrate all too clearly the political manoeuvrings, the back stabbing and the sheer incompetence of both individuals and financial institutions. The net result was the closure of Brittains Paper Mills and the loss of even more jobs. The background to the financial agreement with E.C.I. concerned the deterioration of the paper making plant and the need for modernisation. The position had been apparent for several years and Mallinson, upon his appointment to Managing Director, addressed the problems.

Prior to 1977 Brittains financial advisors had been Ansbachers and Panmure Gordon and although an excellent relationship had developed the company succumbed to pressure from its stockbrokers Panmures and Rusburghs to change to Hambros. Hambros were both professional and cautious and felt it necessary to carry out an investigation of the company before agreeing to become its advisors. Over a period of several months Hambros directors Dennis Cross, Nicholas Craig-Harvey and Michael Sorkin visited Cheddleton on several occasions and also visited most of the other companies within the group. Despite anticipated difficulties Hambros were satisfied with the potential of Brittains Ltd. and agreed to act for the company. By the summer of 1977 a plan had been decided upon that would place the group on a sound financial footing and provide the capital needed to update and improve the Cheddleton Mills. The plans included the sale of Brittains-Riegel to the American partners for cash, the purchase of Wolvercote Paper Mill from Oxford University Press and the raising of up to £2,000,000 in capital.

Following the advice of Hambros, Stuart Mallinson negotiated the sale of Brittains-Riegel and accepted an offer of £1,000,000. The figure was well in excess of the anticipated £600,000 they had hoped for. Wolvercote Paper Mill had been available for several years but failed to attract a buyer because of its consistent losses. It was obvious that the longer Wolvercote remained unsold the less attractive it would become. Brittains had considered the Wolvercote Mill previously and declined to make an offer. Now, with the situation at Wolvercote deteriorating, Brittains could reconsider from a stronger position. The Wolvercote Mill was thought to be in a good condition and the large machine it used would increase the groups range of products.

The first reaction of the Brittains board was that the management of the Oxford University Press, the owners of Wolvercote, lacked financial discipline. With more rigid controls Wolvercote would return to profit and become an attribute to the group. But only if a favourable deal could be struck. To this end Mallinson negotiated a deal with the finance director of O.U.P. David Mitchell. For Brittains it was an excellent deal in which Wolvercote was valued not at market value but, at assets value and the cost of the deal could be met by a combination of shares and cash. Mallinson was wise enough to keep Brittains merchant bankers fully informed of the negotiations surrounding the Wolvercote deal and he had their full approval. On the other hand the management of Oxford University Press failed to keep their own advisors informed and David Mitchell formally accepted the Brittains offer. It was only after the deal was concluded and the press announcement imminent that the O.U.P. advisors became fully conversant with the facts. They immediately condemned the deal and told Mitchell he had given the business away. There may well be some justification in this matter for a valuation of Wolvercote by Walmesleys of Bury assessed its value at £3,000,000.

Brittains had bought it for a song, with a cash payment of £575,000 plus shares valued at about £1,500,000.

Mallinson had now concluded two of their objectives on favourable terms. Brittains-Riegel had been sold for a figure above expectations and Wolvercote had been purchased very cheaply indeed. All that was required now was the injection of capital, and that objective was to prove difficult. Behind the scenes the politicians of industry were working overtime. Mitchell and the O.U.P. were still smarting from the Wolvercote deal and became embroiled with financier E.C.I. in an effort to give credence to their decision to accept the Brittains deal. Initially Hambros had offered financial support to Brittains at a level well below the £2,000,000 required. This, plus the condition that Hambros wished to impose, was not to Brittains liking, and the offer was rejected. Hambros acted with honour and put their weight behind the negotiations with E.C.I. At the same time Peter Maughan of the Bank of England in Manchester suggested that Brittains might also like to consider an alternative source of finance through the N.E.B. Both E.C.I. and N.E.B. were keen to provide Brittains with cash once they had carried out their investigations. Hambros continued to support E.C.I. and E.C.I. themselves were under pressure from the financial press to invest more of their funds. At this stage N.E.B. were considered the bank of last resort.

Brittains, however, kept an open mind and provided each party with an identical corporate plan. The investigation carried out by E.C.I. appeared to be lacking in substance and the personnel concerned seemed anxious to beat N.E.B. in securing the Brittains signatures. The first meeting included Stuart Mallinson and Vic Rickless of Brittains and Tony Lorenz and David Cole of E.C.I. who were both assistants to Alan Barrett the Managing Director. Barrett did not attend. The investigation by Lorenz and Cole centred mainly on the details of the corporate plan and discussions between Cole and Rickless, the financial director of Brittains. Evidently the answers provided by Rickless were satisfactory and shortly afterwards Alan Barrett made his one and only visit to the head office at Cheddleton. The visit was brief indeed considering the amount of money involved and the importance of the investigation. Barrett was to spend less than an hour examining the Brittains set up before speeding off to Manchester for lunch at the Bank of England. He subsequently made a flying visit to Oxford where he spent about an hour at the Wolvercote Mill.

Lorenz was far more thorough and visited Kenmac, the Plant Hire Co. the Builders Supply Co. and Priestners, taking in total just three hours for the visits. This was the extent of the E.C.I. investigation which can only be described as slipshod and casual. A more thorough investigation would have entailed extensive visits to each company within the group, an examination of individual accounts, discussions with key personnel and a precise examination of company balance sheets prior to seeking an explanation of the corporate plan. Brittains themselves carried out a more stringent investigation before purchasing any of their own companies.

Alan Barrett, the Managing Director of E.C.I. was happy enough with the examination and telephoned Brittains Chairman, Ray Latchford, with the good news. E.C.I. were satisfied and the money was available. Brittains, although surprised at the speed of the offer, were delighted to accept. Meantime the examination by N.E.B. was progressing far more slowly. N.E.B. were painstakingly thorough with prolonged visits to every member of the Brittains group. Long and detailed discussions took place between Mallinson and Arthur Ward the director of N.E.B. over items in the corporate plan. Eventually N.E.B. also offered their financial support but as Brittains had verbally committed themselves to E.C.I. they felt obliged to reject the N.E.B. offer. It later transpired that Ward had telephoned Barrett and offered a 50/50 deal with E.C.I. in which they would both contribute £1,000,000. Barrett not only refused the offer but did not inform Brittains either. The sequence of events surrounding the provision of the £2,000,000 was as follows:

22/09/1977	Letter from Mallinson to Hambros asking them to arrange institutional credit.
04/10/1977	Brittains meet O.U.P. to discuss purchase of Wolvercote.
01/11/1977	First meeting with E.C.I.
09/11/1977	Letter from Hambros offering finance of £1.5 million. Rejected because of conditions.
11/11/1977	First meeting with N.E.B.
23/11/1977	Second meeting with N.E.B. and offer of £2 million.
21/12/1977	Letter of intent from E.C.I.

By this time Brittains had been investigated often enough to feel confident that their plans were sound and their intentions honourable. During the negotiations with E.C.I. and N.E.B. Brittains received yet another offer of finance. They were visited by Mr David Nabarro and three of his colleagues from brokers Laurie Millbank of London. Nabarro represented a fairly large shareholder and as such was made welcome on the 28th November 1977. Two weeks later, on the 16th December, Brittains received a visit from John Campbell of Noble Grossart, merchant bankers. Nabarro and Campbell were good friends and the conclusion of the visits was an offer from Noble Grossart to become Brittains merchant bankers and to provide the £2,000,000. From Brittains point of view it was very flattering but far too late and the offer was considered by the board and politely refused.

As 1977 drew to a close the Brittains board acted promptly in bringing details of the years trading up to date. By February a draft copy of the accounts had been prepared and a copy forwarded to E.C.I. The reaction of E.C.I. was nothing short of hysterical. A meeting to discuss the draft accounts was deemed an urgent necessity and the Brittains board was summoned to London on February the 27th 1978.

The main bone of contention was the extraordinary write offs of £700,000 covering the closure of Johnsons and Macclesfield Engineering during the summer of 1977. In actual fact a figure of £600,000 had been quoted as an estimate in the corporate plan. The £600,000 had been noted by N.E.B. and was considered prior to their offer to Brittains. E.C.I. it seems had overlooked the item and now sought to highlight the fact by claiming that they had been deliberately misled. Present at the meeting were:

Latchford, Mallinson and Rickless		Brittains.
T. Barker	-	Auditors Ashworth Moseley.
M. Sorkin, N. Craig-Harvey		Hambros
M. Sayer	-	Solicitors Norton Rose.
Barrett and Cole		E.C.I.

Itemised for discussion ;

1)   The extraordinary item.
2)   The press announcement.
3)   Directors Service Agreement and Bonus arrangements.

Items 2 and 3 were totally ignored. Barrett and Cole arrived thirty minutes late and immediately launched their attack which centred on their annoyance that the Johnsons write off had not been discussed and, as a consequence, any deal with Brittains would be held in abeyance until the whole civil engineering division had been subjected to an independent account investigation. Despite the chorus of protestation from the Brittains representatives and the fact that nothing had been hidden from E.C.I. the meeting failed to reach agreement and broke up acrimoniously having agreed to meet again at 2.30 p.m. Barrett and Cole once again failed to arrive on time and eventually returned to resume the meeting at 3.30 p.m. They had obviously been discussing the mornings events at great length and had decided upon a plan of action for the afternoon. Ignoring the Brittains directors they asked to see Michael Sorkin and spent the rest of the afternoon with him, leaving the other executives to twiddle their thumbs. After some considerable time Sorkin rejoined the rest and told them that Barrett and Cole wanted to withdraw from the deal. Sorkin had resisted strongly and told them that withdrawal was not an option. Barrett and Cole stayed out of sight as Sorkin advised the meeting of the conditions E.C.I. now wished to impose.

1)   An independent accounts investigation into Johnsons and the Civil Engineering Division.
2)   A sale of that division at a later date.
3)   The sale of Priestners, the haulage company.
4)   A cut back in dividends.

Latchford and Mallinson pointed out that the last three items were not part of the deal and therefore unacceptable. Item 1 had already been accepted. At this point Latchford and Mallinson reached the end of their tether and could accept the rudeness of Barrett and Cole no longer. They confronted them and, after words were exchanged, it was agreed that the air needed to be cleared if discussions were to continue. The confrontation went some way to appeasing everyone and Sorkin once again spoke with Barrett and Cole. It was not until 5.30pm that Sorkin returned and advised that item 1 would be the only item to be imposed. Furthermore Sorkin had reduced the investigation period to eight days instead of the several weeks intimated earlier. The final exchanges between Barrett, Cole and the rest of the meeting was hypocritical to say the least. Latchford was assured that no ones integrity was in doubt and that the coming investigation would serve only to make the relationship stronger. Rickless, Mallinson and Latchford could have been forgiven if they doubted the sincerity of such words. What Messrs Sorkin, Sayers and Barker thought is anyone's guess. Following the meeting the independent investigation went ahead at a pace.

28/2/78	M. Sorkin went with E.C.I. to ask Touche Ross to investigate Johnsons and the Civil Engineering Division.
1/3/78	Tony Herron and Bob Jackson of Touche Ross arrived at Cheddleton at 4.15pm to meet Vic Rickless and Tom Barker of Ashworth Moseley and Stuart Mallinson. The meeting continued long into the evening and covered the Johnson position in detail.
2/3/78	Mallinson, Herron, Jackson and Barker meet at Kenmac. A report on Johnsons has been prepared and the situation is again discussed at length. Herron and Jackson profess themselves satisfied and return to London in the afternoon.
3/3/78	Sorkin attends a meeting with Herron and Jackson of Touche Ross and E.C.I. Herron gives E.C.I. a favourable report on Brittains but E.C.I. insist on further investigation after a sum of £40,000 was thought to be accounted for incorrectly.
6/3/78	Jackson visits Kenmore once again and continues the investigation. His final comment to
7/3/78	E.C.I. is that Brittains is all right and that he has no criticism. E.C.I. accept his report.

E.C.I. now had no option but to accept the deal and on the 7th. of March 1978 the agreement was signed in their London office. Even then there was to be a touch of malice. Before the deal could be concluded Latchford and Mallinson were required to sign a paper accepting Touche Ross as joint auditors even though Brittains were perfectly happy with Ashworth Mosley. Brittains felt pressurised to accept. What with the rudeness of Barrett, the enforced acceptance of Touche Ross and the acrimonious background with E.C.I. the agreement did not get off to a good start.

Worse was to come when E.C.I. as part of the Wolvercote deal, appointed David Mitchell as their representative. Under the circumstances Mitchell's appointment was not the most sensitive move. A second director Michael Jackson was also appointed. Mitchell, working away behind the scenes, had given his full support to E.C.I. It was beginning to look very much as though the efforts of Latchford and Mallinson had resulted not in the respect they deserved, but in resentment by Barrett, Cole and Mitchell. A new board was beginning to take shape but the balance of power still remained with Latchford and Mallinson.

An Extraordinary General Meeting of the company was called for 3rd April to ratify the transactions. By now it was obvious to everyone that more was going on outside the meetings than at the meetings themselves. A few days before the E.G.M. Stuart Mallinson received a telephone call from Mr Nabarro to say that he and others were unhappy about the announced deals. They thought Wolvercote was a bad purchase and recounted all the stories they had heard about old machinery and the difficulties O.U.P. had had in finding a buyer. Mallinson corrected the impression and Nabarro appeared satisfied. However, Nabarro went on to say that the investors he represented were unhappy with the fact that E.C.I. would be controlling a large slice of Brittains. Nabarro declared that he could muster a 25 % voting opposition at the E.G.M. and so stop the resolution from being passed. He offered once again to put a package together that would provide Brittains with £1,000,000. This was obviously not enough and the proposal was far too late anyway. It took another high powered meeting at Hambros in London to resolve matters. The meeting over two days involved Mallinson, Sorkin, Craig-Harvey, Nabarro and Campbell (of Noble Grossart). They were later joined by Martin Cooke of Rensburghs. Cooke's inclusion had not been expected. He had always had a sound relationship with Brittains so his inclusion with the opposition came as something of a surprise. He may well have been upset at being denied access to Brittains-Riegel at a time when negotiations were at a sensitive stage. Whatever the reason he now gave his support to Nabarro. The long and protracted meeting eventually resulted in Nabarro supporting Brittains at the E.G.M. but at a price. Nabarro wanted a representative on the Brittains board. This was to be a W. Houston. The Extraordinary General Meeting went without a hitch and Brittains now had three new non-executive directors on the main board:

David Mitchell: Formally in charge of finance at Oxford University Press and responsible for the sale of the Wolvercote Mill to Brittains Ltd. The Brittains board were not impressed with Mitchell.

Michael Jackson: Inherited a family business employing up to 200 people. The business was sold to Ozalid who appointed Jackson a non-executive director. It was at Ozalid that Michael Jackson met Alan Barrett of E.C.I.

Bill Houston: Bill Houston had served in the Royal Navy before going into industry where he gained the confidence of a number of city contacts.

It was the general opinion of the Brittains board that the three new directors were not of the calibre expected. They lacked experience at senior level and were unfamiliar with the running of a public company the size of the Brittains group. Like it or not the directors of Brittains Ltd who had long experience of running a group consisting of around twenty companies were slowly but surely being replaced by nominee directors whose experience was more financial than hands on.

The trading position of Brittains Ltd changed dramatically between April and August of 1978. Sales were well below expectations with Kenmac and Brittains Paper being particularly badly hit. Kenmac, usually so successful, found themselves with two contracts that had run into difficulties and were losing money. Under normal circumstances Kenmac could have completed the contracts and then looked for better deals. Such events were not unknown in civil engineering and Kenmac had ridden storms before and still managed to build up a good track record. On this occasion time was running out fast.

With Brittains Paper it was a different story. The high levels of expenditure had caused a sharp rise in the break-even point and the need for trade was desperate. A dramatic collapse of the market in four prime areas created even more havoc with the budget. Rizla, the cigarette paper company, experienced a serious problem with its paper mill in France and suddenly halved its requirement from Brittains Paper. At the same time the Brittains Paper Mills main product line, capacitor tissue, which previously enjoyed around two thirds of the home market, suddenly dropped to 25%. On the overseas market, Tervakoski, having lost most of the Russian market reduced prices by 30%. The results were catastrophic and highlighted even more clearly the need for Brittains Ltd. to update and improve its paper making facilities. Whether or not E.C.I., the non-executive directors and the large shareholders would keep their nerve remained to be seen. The objectives remained the same despite the loss of trade and the liquidity problems caused by the cash flow shortfall, eg:

1) Rebuild the best capacitor tissue machine enabling it to run faster, cheaper and more competitively. It would also be able to produce paper for the lucrative American market. The rebuilt machine was expected to be the second biggest in the world.

2) Rebuild the best carbonising machine, based on the acclaimed Braunsteins of France design. This would give Brittains a machine as good as any in the world and one that was capable of high quality production.

3) Modify the Duplex paper machine to enable it to produce Simplex paper. This would remove the need to purchase Simplex paper from Tullis Russel.

During the period when trade was at its worst, Mallinson attempted to keep Barrett and Cole informed and encourage their ongoing support. Both were invited to visit Cheddleton in June but neither accepted the offer. Mallinson was unable to have a conversation with either of them about the trading problems or company strategy. Michael Jackson attended board meetings from May onwards and Houston attended his first board meeting on the 8th of September. No record of dissension appears to have been made. Just what their brief was is anybody's guess although it is obvious that E.C.I., Nabarro and others were only too aware of events, confidential or otherwise.

During May of 1978 Brittains received an informal approach by an interested party, a company around five times larger than them. The larger group contained a small, successful paper making concern and in the event of a take-over of Brittains the paper making concerns would be merged. The company, cash rich and looking for expansion, offered exciting

Priestners Haulage - a
subsidiary of Brittains.

Below
Papermaking at Cheddleton

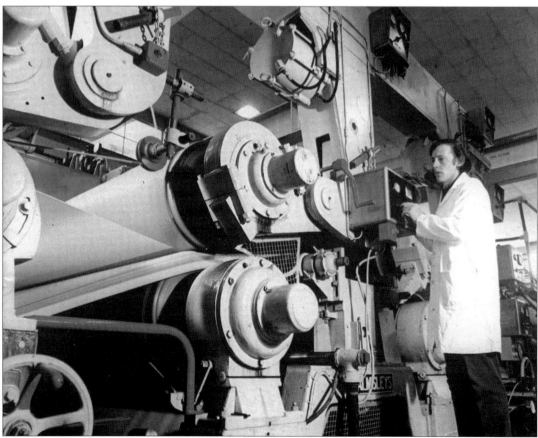

prospects and security for the Cheddleton Mills. With Latchford about to retire, Mallinson would be offered a seat on the main board and be responsible for the Brittains group including the paper making. Several discreet meetings were held between the chairman, the managing director and two main board directors of the larger company and Latchford and Mallinson of Brittains Ltd. Brittains financial situation was discussed frankly and a later visit by a paper making consultant confirmed the fact that huge sums of money needed to be spent. Past experience, when an old mill had pulled the group into a loss, deterred them from going further and they withdrew their interest in September without submitting a formal approach.

The state of affairs within the Brittains board was unsatisfactory to say the least. The non-executive directors were not trusted and the informal approach was deliberately withheld from them on the basis that Barrett and Cole could have used the approach for their own ends and severed their agreement. The intention was to advise Barrett and Cole if and when a formal approach was made. In reality Barrett and Cole of E.C.I. Nabarro and all the other institutional parties were constantly in touch with each other and monitoring events closely. Information from outside the financial circle added fuel to the fire. One particular letter sent to Nabarro by an injured party was quick to give a harsh opinion of Latchford, Mallinson and several other directors. Nails were being hammered into the Brittains' coffin.

In July of 1978, Stuart Mallinson went on holiday. Profits had fallen well below expectations and liquidity was becoming desperate. The informal approach, whilst at this stage still active, was beginning to cool. Despite the fact that the plans for Brittains Paper were sound the doubts of the financiers were increasing. At this point the effective management of the Brittains Group by Stuart Mallinson virtually ended. A meeting in London between Barrett and the non-executive directors decided that Mallinson should go. The lack of trust of the non-executive directors was vindicated. Neither Latchford nor the rest of the executive board were aware of the meeting. Another meeting took place and Latchford and Rickless were summoned to London to attend at the Hambros office. Also at the meeting were Barrett, Cole, Sorkin and Craig-Harvey. Barrett broke the news of Mallinsons removal, supporting his decision with criticisms from suppliers, customers, institutions and investors who considered Mallinson to be a very bad managing director. No doubt comments from past directors and employees formed part of his opinion. Conversely Mallinson, had he been there, would have been justified in pointing out just how much support those same people had given him not so long ago. At the same meeting Latchford revealed details of the informal approach and suggested that they should see if it reached fruition. This single action probably saved Latchfords career. His own neck was on the block even though he was only a few months away from retirement. An ignominious end was the last thing he wanted. He had been at Brittains man and boy and had built up a reputation as a man of honour and distinction.

Upon Mallinsons return from holiday Latchford told him of the decision to dismiss him. The rest of the board had not yet been informed - officially. The meetings of the Brittains board that followed registered support and sympathy for Mallinson. Sandy Wright put forward a proposal that the board's support should be included in the minutes of the meeting. The proposal could find no seconders. The rest of the board were more concerned for their own jobs than saving Mallinson. Mallinsons next move was to suggest a private meeting between himself and the non-executive directors at which he would seek a vote of confidence. Latchford refused point blank to support such a move. Barrett had told him that if the Brittains board refused to remove Stuart Mallinson, then the whole board would be removed at an extraordinary general meeting. The threat was followed up formally in writing. Latchford had little trouble persuading his fellow directors that there was no point in the whole board being sacrificed if Stuart Mallinson was to go anyway. Mallinson, now fighting for survival, attended a meeting with the non-executive directors on the 8th of September. He went to great lengths to justify his policies and to defend his decisions on diversification which E.C.I. had described as ridiculous. It is an indisputable fact that despite the successes or failures, most of the diversification programme was carried out under the control of Latchford and Holmes prior to 1973. It is also a fact that many of the diversification deals involved shares rather than excessive amounts of cash and that the share earnings had increased by around 90% in ten years. His pleas fell on stony ground. The final act in the dismissal of Stuart Mallinson took place on the 22nd of September 1978 at a meeting in the London office of Hambros. Present at the meeting were ;

C. Sporburg	Chairman Hambros
N. Craig-Harvey	Hambros
A.N. Other	Hambros
K.R. Latchford	Brittains
S. Mallinson	Brittains
A. Barrett	E.C.I.
D. Cole	E.C.I.
D. Nabarro	Laurie Millbank
M. Cooke	Rensburghs
J. Campbell	Noble Grossart
Lord McGowan	Panmure Gordon

The meeting had been arranged to enable Stuart Mallinson to put his case to E.C.I. and their supporting institutional representatives. It turned out that the supporting representatives were none other than Nabarro of Laurie Millbank and Cooke of Rensburgh. The very people who, back in March, had tried to obstruct the E.C.I. deal and offered Mallinson an alternative. Mallinson, to all intents and purposes, was now dead. The meeting, farcical as it may be, now went ahead. Lord McGowan offered moral support, Latchford distanced himself both physically and vocally and Barrett spoke of a total dishonouring of forecasts and a profligate use of cash. Mallinson, now fighting an impossible battle, not only refuted such allegations but called them emotive and ill informed. He received some support from Campbell but none from the rest of the meeting who listened in silence as Barrett continued with a attack on the diversification companies. His final comments were that Mallinson should go as soon as possible and that all the non-paper making activities should be sold off within a six to twelve month period. The final resolution demanding the departure of Stuart Mallinson was signed on the 3rd of October 1978.

Latchford, anxious to bring his own time to an honourable conclusion was not about to rock the boat. He fixed Mallinsons compensation at a lower level than that recommended by Hambros and Norton Rose. Mallinson's own advisors, furious at the revised figure, were unhappy with the deal. Such was the animosity of Slaughter and May that they advised Mallinson not to sign a single document until the money was actually in his bank account. The departure was acrimonious to the bitter end. It was only at 4.30 p.m. that Mallinson was allowed to contact subsidiary directors and friends and say his goodbyes.

With Mallinson's departure and the imminent departure of Latchford the appointment of a new managing director should have been a vital and urgent necessity. For reasons best known only to Barrett and Co. no appointment was made. Brittains Ltd entered what was to be the final stage of its existence managed by a small board of mainly non-executive directors whos strings were pulled from London. A lack of management skill must surely have been evident. Despite Barrett's claim that three candidates were under consideration the M.D.'s job remained vacant.

Companies within the group were now sold off at an alarming rate for prices that can only be described as give away. It is questionable whether the directors acted with the best interest of the shareholders. They certainly showed no interest for the bewildered employees of an old and respected company. Kenmac which cost £900,000 in 1971 and returned excellent profits with the exception of 1978 was sold for £100,000 plus its current overdraft. This was under-selling at its worst. A true value would have been around £1,000,000.

Priestners towards the end of 1978 was said to have had net assets of £800,000 after deducting money owed to creditors, hire purchase agreements and overdrafts. Its fixed assets included 12 acres of freehold land and 5.5 acres of leasehold sites. Of this 3.2 acres freehold and 5.5 acres leasehold formed part of the Carrington depot. The Carrington depot occupied a prime site adjacent to the Shell refinery in Greater Manchester. The site included 44,000 square feet of modern distribution warehousing and 6,240 square feet of garaging and offices. Priestners also owned 50,000 square feet of warehousing on a freehold site at Dunham-Massey three miles away. In terms of vehicles the company had 60 heavy tractor units valued at £1,000,000 plus, and over 100 trailer units and 30 vans. Additionally it owned a site of several acres at Knottingley with hard standing for vehicles. This site alone, with its position on the junction of the A1(M) and the M62 was worth a considerable amount. The overall value of Priestners was enough to cover the group debts and possible refurbishing costs of Brittains Ltd several times over. Obviously it was an asset worth hanging onto rather than selling. But what an asset! If the details to hand about Priestners are true why on earth was it sold for a mere £365,000. Did anyone visit the site? Did anyone care? This appears to be 'incompetence' on a grand scale.

Brittains Plant was sold for £200,000. No valuation was made of the business. Brittains Building Supplies was put into receivership when the existing management was actively negotiating to buy it. Brittains Insurance Brokers in August 1978 was showing a pre tax profit of £50,000 and had cash in hand of £300,000. It is believed to have been sold for a very small sum, well below its real worth.

Brittains Plastics in 1978 was an excellent company occupying a first rate factory. Over seven years the company increased its capacity many times. Over those years average pre tax profits were £160,000 per annum. Under decent trading conditions a profit of £200,000 per annum would have been possible. The company had assets of almost £500,000. It was sold for just £350,000. Add the costs run up by the so called experts to the poor returns from the sale of the group companies and the incompetence of management begins to look alarming:

Consultancy costs	£ 30,000	
Directors compensation	£ 74,000	
Accountancy charges	£200,000	(1978/79)
Lawyers charges	£ 30,000	
	£334,000	

What little was made from the sale of the companies was spent elsewhere. The money finally obtained from the sales was not sufficient to save the rest of the group from going into receivership. Barclays Bank had had a long and trusting relationship with Brittains both as a paper making concern and as a group. Managing Directors had built up a good rapport and the bank managers were regular visitors to Brittains. They had supported the company through good times and bad and knew the business far better than E.C.I. They knew nothing of Mallinsons dismissal until after it had happened. What they did know was that the policy and strategy they understood and supported for years was being changed overnight.

With confidence eroded Barclays decided to withdraw. They called in the overdraft only to discover that what they feared was true. The money to repay them was not available. Receivers were appointed in January 1979 after the directors had asked the bank to intervene. Brittains Paper Mills were bankrupt and over a period of twenty months Jordans and Cork-Gully completed the onerous task of winding up the affairs of the company. The final accounts dated 25th of October 1980 make sorry reading.

Assets	£695,629	
Liabilities	£3,862,222	Secured Creditors and Debenture holders.
	£2,514,241	Unsecured Creditors.
	£533,804	Preferential Creditors.
	£6,910,266	

What became of the £2,000,000 lent by E.C.I. is difficult to say. A cynic could be forgiven for suspecting that it was recovered although it is impossible to reach such a conclusion. To the good people of Cheddleton it must all have seemed like a game in which they were the pawns. Expendable and of little consequence. With the aftermath of the collapse comes the wisdom of hindsight and even then opinion is divided. The most frequent question is " Would it have been wiser to have simply remained a paper manufacturer?"

The answer is far from simple. The chances are that without the diversification, paper making would have continued at Cheddleton but on a much smaller scale, with a smaller workforce and redundancies would still have occurred. To continue to expand and compete on a global scale vast sums of money would have been required. Brittains main competition, Kores Vienna, Gunther Wagner and Gehar and Braunstein were taking more and more of the market with faster machinery and improved technology. It is doubtful whether Brittains would have had the muscle to compete without huge injections of capital and the inevitable inclusion of finance house representatives on its board of directors. Change was inevitable.

Many of the businesses within the group were sold as going concerns although the acumen of the sellers raises a few questions. Kenmac for example was sold for £100,000 plus its overdraft of £350,000. This, despite profits approaching £250,000. Virtually all of the paper making units within the group were snapped up and remain profitable to this day. The Hanley mill, Brittains Converters, was purchased by Tullis Russell the Scottish paper makers who were quick to recognise the potential of both the business and the management. Brittains Plastics at Smallthorne continues to go from strength to strength. Other manufacturers quickly took up the slack. Wiggins Teape now produce more lightweight airmail paper than ever and the paper for cigarettes has expanded rapidly in the Far east. In short the demand for paper continues to defy the advent of computers, word processors and printers.

Alfred Haigh was correct when he advised the Ministry of Labour in 1949 that the coming decades would bring great changes to the paper industry. Even he could not have envisaged just how great that change would be.

Composition of the Group

HOLDING COMPANY

BRITTAINS LIMITED
Cheddleton, Leek Staffs.

OPERATING SUBSIDIARY COMPANIES

(wholly owned except where stated)

BRITTAINS (GROUP MANAGEMENT) LIMITED
Cheddleton, Leek, Staffs.

BRITTAINS (GROUP ESTATES) LIMITED
Cheddleton, Leek, Staffs.

Owns industrial property used by fellow subsidiary companies.

PAPER

BRITTAINS PAPER LIMITED
Cheddleton, Leek, Staffs.,
Overseas branch office
Osaka, Japan.

Manufacture of speciality tissues.

Sells the Group's paper products and allied products of other manufacturers.

BRITTAINS CONVERTERS LIMITED
Hanley, Stoke-on-Trent.

Manufacture of specialised coated papers particularly for the decalcomania industry.

BRITTAINS-ARBORFIELD LIMITED
Helpston, Peterborough

Manufacture of technical speciality papers including hospital sterilisable papers, bookbinding, envelope manillas, M.G. liner papers and laminated board.

BRITTAINS PAPER AND PACKAGING LIMITED
Hanley, Stoke-on-Trent

Paper and Film Merchants.

ALLAN B. CARLISLE & SONS (1969) LIMITED
Macclesfield, Cheshire

Manufacture of specialised coated papers.

BRITTAINS HOSPITAL SUPPLIES LIMITED
Cheddleton, Leek, Staffs.

Sells the Group's specialised products to hospitals at home and overseas.

BRITTAINS PAPERS INCORPORATED
Stamford Connecticut
Registered in the U.S.A.

Sells the Group's paper products in the U.S.A. and Canada.

BRITTAINS (AUSTRALASIA) PTY. LIMITED
Sydney, New South Wales
Registered in Australia

Sells the Group's paper products in Australia.

PLASTICS

BRITTAINS PLASTICS LIMITED
Smallthorne, Stoke-on-Trent

Extrusion of polythene film and manufacture of polythene bags.

Composition of the Group (continued)

LIGHT ENGINEERING

MACCLESFIELD ENGINEERING LIMITED
Stockport, Greater Manchester

Light engineering, general engineering and sheet metal work.

HOLTSCHOPPEN UND BRITTAINS G.m.b.H.
Viersen, Germany
Registered in Germany

An agency company in Western Germany selling engineering products (50% owned).

CIVIL ENGINEERING

KENMAC CONSTRUCTION CO. LIMITED
Sandiway, Cheshire

Civil Engineering contractors, specialising in sewer and pipe laying and the building of sewerage works, effluent plants and waterworks and industrial buildings.

KENMAC CONSTRUCTION (JERSEY) LIMITED
Jersey, Channel Islands
Registered in Jersey

KENMAC CONSTRUCTION (GUERNSEY) LIMITED
Guernsey, Channel Islands
Registered in Guernsey

BRITTAINS TUNNELLING LIMITED
Sandiway, Cheshire

Civil Engineering contractors, specialising in tunnelling.

BRITTAINS BUILDERS SUPPLIES LIMITED
Warrington, Cheshire

Merchants of building and allied materials.

BRITTAINS PLANT LIMITED
Warrington, Cheshire

Hires moveable plant to companies in the Group and to other users.

HAULAGE

G. PRIESTNER LIMITED
Carrington, Greater Manchester

Operates a transport and warehousing service.

INSURANCE BROKING and FREIGHT

BRITTAINS INSURANCE BROKERS LIMITED
Manchester

Insurance Broking.

BRITTAINS WORLD FREIGHT LIMITED
Manchester

Forwarding and Shipping Agents.

TOP ROW
LEFT TO RIGHT   R. COGHILL   W. GIBSON   H. NEWNHAM   A. STEVENTON   W. CLOWES   H. BROWN

A.R. MALGARY   H. HOLLINS   E. PICKFORD   W. BURNDRED   C. BROWN   J. MACHIN   J. SHENTON

M. HEAPEY   B. HALL   S. ALCOCK   G. CARTLIDGE   H.H. WELLER   F.S. GLEW   F. BURROWS   K. JOHNSTON   V. EDGE

Engineering Division at Brittain's 1950s.

Brittain's Ltd 1896.

Max Chadwick

Ward 13's verandah
(female admission
ward) early 1950s
(Sister Connolly, S/N
Milne, Student Nurse
Colacicci).

Below:
New Admission Ward
about 1950.

Below:
The main drive into
St Edward's Hospital.

St Edwards Hospital

Chapter Eight
St. Edward's Hospital: Nurse Vera Gibson 1960-1973

The walk through the village and along the hospital drive was pleasant enough but it was a nervous twenty year old who approached the Matron's office. In those days the Matron ran the female side of the hospital and it was she who would decide my fate. She was a small grey-haired lady with her hair pulled straight back. With thick lensed spectacles and a Scottish accent she was forbidding enough to deter anyone. I gained the impression that she never went outside, let alone enjoyed herself. She very quickly decided that I was not really suitable for nursing. She commented that I would not like the patients or cope with the work for very long, but I could have a go as they were desperate for staff. With that the interview terminated - it was obvious she had more important things to do than talk to the likes of me. I was determined to earn some money and my desperation quickly displaced my dented pride.

One week later I had been for the medical examination and was accepted as their youngest trainee. I was to learn subsequently that, by this time, only the chronically sick or the insane failed the medical - so you either passed or joined the others inside! My next call was to the sewing room where I was measured for my uniform. This was a hive of activity with treadle sewing machines going hell for leather and piles of linen everywhere. The staff, with the help of several patients, made up sheets, pillow cases, clothes and uniforms. After much discussion and two attempts I was considered measured and a uniform of the appropriate size was produced. I tried it on and thought glumly of a saying of my grandmother's, "It fits where it touches". Secretly I reached the conclusion that the measuring process could easily be omitted.

The uniform consisted of a plain cotton dress, pink in colour, with starched white cuffs and a starched white collar that buttoned onto the dress and immediately chafed the back of my neck. Next came a bibbed apron, also starched, and a starched cap which was ironed flat and impossible to fold. With some effort and several hair pins I donned this head piece and clipped an elastic belt around my waist to hold everything together. It was totally impractical for the work we did, but I loved it. I already felt like a proper nurse. I had a sense of belonging, even though I was new to the job.

I spent my first month, as all new nurses did, on the sick ward which also acted as a reception ward for geriatric patients. On my first day I kept my back to the wall whenever possible and constantly checked the position of the exits for a quick getaway. I was firmly convinced the patients would attack me. But by the second day I began to realise that most of the patients were too ill to sit up in bed unaided never mind find the energy to attack me. The sister was very patient and kind to everyone, and she began to teach me the basics of psychiatric nursing. This motherly woman had all the manner of a married woman and I was surprised to learn that she was in fact single and lived with another sister. The relationship was often the source of speculation and innuendo, but it was of no consequence to me. I grew to like her very much and it was with some regret that my month came to a close.

After my honeymoon on the sick ward I was dispatched to other wards. The worst was the dreaded Ward 19. Dreaded not so much for the ward or the patients as for the sister. This tall imposing figure ran Ward 19 with a rod of iron and did not suffer fools gladly. My arrival was greeted with, "Who are you? Why can't they send me someone who is of use to me?"

I quietly settled in and set about my first duties which were to sit all the old ladies up in bed for their breakfasts. The breakfast of porridge, egg sandwiches and a cup of tea had to be administered and consumed in ten minutes flat if Sister's wrath was to be avoided. I quickly learned that Sister liked to see clean plates and woe betide us if any scraps were left when she entered the dormitory. I also learned that the secret of a clean plate was to throw away any scraps through the nearest window which explained why the birds sang so cheerfully outside Ward 19. We were more afraid of Sister than we were of the patients dying from malnutrition. It took very little to upset her. On one occasion I saw her throw a large, heavy fireguard at one nurse who had displeased her.

What my friend Sheila and I did to gain her favour I do not know but she suddenly took a shine to us. This was bad enough, but worse was to come; every morning she cooked both of us an egg for breakfast. Her method was to fry the eggs in a sea of butter and produce a concoction that neither of us had the courage to refuse. We sat there, forcing the sickly eggs down our throats and hoping fervently that someone else would be her favourites.

Some time later I went up in the world and was dispatched to the Admission Block which stood alone some distance from the main block. Inside it was far more pleasant than the average ward at St Edwards. The wards were small and contained either two or four beds, and there were side rooms, a comfortable day room and a modern kitchen. About thirty ladies were there and for the most part they were suffering from various forms of depression; some had had a nervous breakdown and a teenager had just been diagnosed as having schizophrenia.

Twice a week the patients were given E.C.T. or Electro-Convulsive Therapy. E.C.T. involved passing an electric current through to the brain to stimulate it. No-one seemed to know how it worked exactly but the result on some of the patients was very good indeed. The treatment on two occasions was given 'neat' which meant that neither an anaesthetic or a muscle relaxant was administered. It was frightening to watch as the patient went into a violent muscle spasm and God alone knows what it was like to receive. I am pleased to say that I witnessed the end of the treatment in this way in about 1960.

Shortly after I started on the 'Admissions' I was asked to accompany a social worker on a trip to Leek. We had been asked to collect an old lady who could no longer look after herself and had been found on the streets confused and not knowing where she was. Our visit began quite well. We located her little terraced house and she let us in. We had a cup of tea with her, talked to her and explained that we wanted to take her into hospital to be looked after. She gathered a few things together and came back with us in the car quite willingly. Once in the ward an older, senior nurse, took over. The old lady, whose name was Sarah, had to be given a bath. This meant of course that she had to be undressed and we soon discovered that she had three lots of underwear on which were all held together with large safety pins. The nurse, obviously impatient, simply could not be bothered with all the safety pins. She began tugging at the clothes, ripping them away and shouting at Sarah to co-operate. Within minutes Sarah was crying and frightened, and in a 'right state'. I am sure I would have reacted the same way had I been treated like that. Occasionally you came across a nurse who was not in the right profession for whatever reason. I think she was one of them. About three months later this nurse was admitted to the psychiatric ward of a nearby general hospital suffering from depression. Perhaps my hasty judgment of her was misplaced.

When we admitted patients, normally, apart from cosmetic items, all personal belongings were taken from them. This included cigarettes and lighters and usually created a bad mood and a lack of co-operation from the outset. Let's face it, most of them had come to us reluctantly and immediately taking away their cigarettes was not very clever. Thankfully the rules were later relaxed somewhat. Nursing chronic patients, psychiatric or geriatric, was not always very rewarding as few showed any sign of improvement or recovery, but on 'Admissions' many did recover.

One Saturday I took a few patients to sit outside. The majority of the ward had gone home for the weekend and those that were left just sat with me on the benches and talked. They talked to each other, and to me, about their problems, and we spent a pleasant afternoon idling our time away. I did not think much about it until later that evening when two or three of them told me and the other staff how they had enjoyed the afternoon and how much the talking had helped them. I suppose it was a simple form of counselling, ahead of its time, had we but realised. It taught me that a lot of the time the best way to help people was to find time to listen to them.

In the main hospital there was still a number of padded cells. A sort of orange coloured rubber covered the floor and walls of the windowless rooms. Patients who became very violent and uncontrollable were stripped naked and locked in the cell until they calmed down. Some, the really difficult ones, were manhandled into straight jackets with their arms strapped tightly to their body. In the days before the introduction of modern drugs I gather this was a common practice. The patients could spend several days, or even a week, in the padded cell and were left alone except when a group of nurses cleaned the room or force fed them. It really was a very cruel practice. I must admit that without drugs some patients were extremely violent and frightening to be with but they did not deserve to be put in a padded cell. Like the 'neat' E.C.T., padded cells were phased out during the early 1960's.

One patient called Martha was immensely strong. When she was in a manic state the nurses said she had the strength of three and I can vouch that this was very true. Most of the time Martha was no trouble to anyone and would behave normal for weeks at a time. But then her mood would change. The warning of the mood change came when Martha began to sing, "There'll be bluebirds over the white cliffs of Dover". This was a sure sign she was about to 'go off'. Once the singing began we had about two minutes to guide her into a side room and lock the door until she calmed down.

On this particular day I was in the linen room at the bottom of the dormitory sorting out the sheets when I heard Martha. She was walking down the dormitory singing the dreaded song. I had nowhere to escape and I felt myself break into a cold sweat. I remembered only too clearly how, a few weeks earlier, she had bitten a nurses leg so severely that it needed several stitches to close the wound. The nurse still has the scar. I kept very still and silent as Martha slowly approached the linen room. In what seemed like a lifetime she went past the linen room then turned and went back into the dormitory just in time for the other nurses to grab her and lock her in a side room. I sat there shaking and thankful of my narrow escape.

Sorting out the linen was all part of the job as was the bed making prior to Matron's inspection. Of course the patients had to be fed and their medication administered, but even this was a low priority as far as Sister was concerned. Everything was put on hold while the ward was made pristine. Tidiness and uniformity took over. Sheets were turned down by the exact amount and tucked in with the patient lying flat. Counterpanes were smoothed with all the corners folded in exactly the same manner. Beds had to be in a straight line and the locker tops cleared. In short the whole ward had to look perfect, with the patients playing a secondary role and not daring to put an arm out of bed.

Matron was quick to point out any faults to Sister, who was even quicker to reprimand us. With Matron's departure came a sigh of relief and a well earned cup of tea. It was some relief to all of us when a more patient-friendly regime was introduced in later years.

Later I was moved onto the easier wards, where the patients could walk and no heavy lifting was required, and my friend Sheila and I quickly got on top of the work. We had a very strict sister but it was a sunny day and she was in a good mood, so she she sent us into what was called the courts, a garden enclosed by iron railings. We were told to plant out boxes of bedding plants and as we both liked gardening we enjoyed ourselves, chatting as we worked. But it was all short lived. Later in the day a patient began to play up and Sister's good mood quickly evaporated. She came outside and bellowed at us, shouting something to the effect that the plants had better all be planted or else. Of course they were not, but Sheila had a bright idea. Digging a large hole she buried the remaining plants in one place. For weeks I worried, imagining a great mass of flowers all appearing in one spot with very few elsewhere. But eventually nature did us proud and Sister made no comment.

Despite the fact that the courts were supposed to enable the female patients to enjoy the fresh air without meeting the male patients, it was not foolproof. Sister told of how once, when some of her patients were in the court, a male patient, although unable to get past the high railings which were only 4 inches apart, still managed to have intercourse with one of the ladies through the railings! This of course proved beyond doubt her constant warnings for vigilance. Sister was always pointing out the lady who had committed such a terrible sin, a small, thin lady who seemed incapable of washing or dressing, let alone having intercourse. She immediately went up in our estimation - we just hoped she had enjoyed the experience, because there was little chance of her repeating it. It is difficult to believe that, by 1970, female staff were looking after male patients, and male staff female patients, progress that most people welcomed.

During the 1960s TB (tuberculosis) was still common and we nursed these patients in Ward 17. This was an unusual ward because it consisted of two sides. The day room, Sister's office, a clinic room, a kitchen and store rooms on one side and a corridor leading to the dormitory and beds for geriatrics on the other. From the beds you could reach the verandah which housed ten beds where patients were left to benefit from the fresh air. When we were short of bed space in the ward we transferred patients to the verandah as a stop gap. Awkward patients also found themselves on the verandah benefiting from the effects of a force nine gale or a winter's chill! The fresh air, which was supposed to help the disease, was more likely to result in pneumonia. There was also a barrier nursing method which was supposed to eliminate the spread of tuberculosis. I always thought the successful treatment of this deadly disease in the late sixties was quite wonderful, although people seemed to take it for granted.

My favourite patient at that time, and of many other nurses, was called Florence May. Florrie, or May as we called her, was well into her seventies when I nursed her. She was tall, with straight grey hair held back with a slide. She was quite ordinary until she smiled. She had the most beautiful smile which lit up her whole face. One smile from Florrie and you

Author

Above:
Summer house in
the hospital
grounds.

Right:
Malloy House.

Below:
The main
corridor.

Author

Author

Mrs P. Harris

Three young St Edward's nurses

Below: The Main Hall with stage.

Below:
Occupational Therapy

Author

forgave her anything and everything. Florrie lived in her own little world, dwelling in the past. She talked about her son James as if he was still ten years old and would describe dressing him in a blue velvet jacket with a lace collar, and velvet trousers to match. She would speak of Sunday afternoons outings and how proud she was of him.

As she suffered from dementia she could be quite a handful at times and would occasionally be secured in a side room, whether for her own protection or that of the other patients I cannot remember. On one occasion I went into the side room to give her some tea only to discover that she had wet herself. Her nightie and the sheets were absolutely soaked and she had stripped everything off and was struggling to hold onto her clothes in one corner of the room. I asked her what she was doing and she told me that she was putting them through the mangle as they had got a little damp and did I want anything.

For a time Florrie was moved to an upstairs ward. As this was her first experience of a first floor room I went to see how she was settling in and if she liked it. "Oh yes" she said, looking through the window. Outside the tall trees were in full leaf and looking beautiful. She looked at the trees and said "I am sitting in the tree tops, would you sit with me? Isn't it lovely?"

She was such a mixture of personalities. She could be very destructive at times, fighting with other patients or throwing her dinner on the floor if she had a mind to. Then she would throw her arms around you, smile and tell you how bonny you looked. Without really knowing it Florrie could twist the staff round her little finger. I admit she was spoiled and Florrie got away with more than most patients.

Later I was introduced to Ward 23, which at that time was still locked. The large key that I had been given when I was first enrolled was now essential - once inside the doors were self-locking. As they banged behind me I always felt that it was similar to prison. I am sure that the patients must have felt the same. I can still recall the smell you encountered when entering such wards. The smell was not identifiable as a single offensive odour but was a mixture with pine disinfectant predominant, plus the clinical smell you encounter in all hospitals. Mingling with it all was the unmistakable stench of urine. No matter how often we bathed the patients and gave them fresh clothes, and no matter how much effort you put into cleaning the ward, you could never eliminate the smell of urine. It was as though over the years it had penetrated the fabric of the ward. It seemed to be deep in the woodwork and brickwork where no amount of cleaning could reach it.

During the day time, although you had your fifty of sixty patients to look after, there was an overlap with the changing shift which meant an increase in staff for a while. This enabled us to use the time to take the patients for a walk around the grounds or to visit the hospital cinema or simply to talk to them. The worst part of the day came at 5.00 p.m. when the day staff left and the late shift carried on alone.

Sister, with the help of two or three sensible patients, would serve tea in the dining room to all the able bodied. Two nurses were then sent to the dormitory to feed the bed patients. One particular sister who was very strict gave us an allotted time to feed approximately twenty ladies. They were sick and very old, some were contracted and often quite restive. It seemed to me that what we needed was lots of time and not an impossible deadline. But that sums up one side of nursing at that time. A limited number of staff with patients to feed, beds to tidy, wards to clean and baths to be given. There was hardly time for a more relaxed regime.

Ward 23 was situated in the far corner of the hospital. An appropriate sign above the door may have been "Out of sight out of mind". It was approached by means of a dingy, poorly lit corridor and was very easy to miss. In fact it was conveniently missed quite often, especially when important visitors, such as the Mayor, local councilors and hospital governors were being given the guided tour. This was because the patients in Ward 23 were generally suffering from severe psychiatric disorder which caused them to behave in a disruptive or violent manner which may well have embarrassed our eminent visitors.

They were obviously aware that we housed such patients but the hospital management did not think visitors should be subjected to seeing them at close quarters. I must admit that the ward was not a popular one because of the number of volatile or just unpleasant patients. But this was more than compensated for by the wonderful staff on that ward; I was only to discover this in the course of time. The first day I arrived for duty I had to use my key to gain entry. I went into the staff room to put my belongings into a locker and to collect a clean apron. As I was in the process of doing this I heard someone with a strong Scottish accent speaking to the patients in a very loud voice. I found the day room and saw the Sister in the doorway. She was obviously the one with the load voice and Scottish accent. Tall, slender and quite severe looking I placed her in her late forties. She was in the process of giving the patients a lecture on how she expected them to behave towards each other and explaining just what would happen if they did not follow her advice. This was Sister Cameron. I looked at her and then at the disgruntled patients - and I thought "I don't think I am going to like it here". How wrong can you be? She needed her loud voice to let them know periodically who was the boss, to ensure the ward ran smoothly. I soon discovered that Cameron was the most caring nurse I had ever worked with. She went to endless trouble trying to make their quality of life better and worked on the basis that this was their home and not just a hospital. Most of the patients were completely institutionalised and could expect to spend the rest of their lives here. Improving their living conditions was Sister Cameron's priority. She always said that no-one should die alone and she always ensured that a very sick or dying patient was moved to a single room. There she was allocated a nurse full time no matter how short staffed we may have been. I saw her do battle with Matron on many occasions, fighting to get an extra nurse and making sure an old lady without relatives or friends did not spend her last hours alone.

Like most wards, 23 was extremely overcrowded and, although it was hospital policy to reduce numbers, we found in practice it never happened. Our solution was far more practical but would have given Matron a seizure. When a patient died or was transferred we acted with lightening speed. First we stripped the bed and removed the mattress. Then we sneaked the mattress and the dismantled bed down the back staircase that led from the dormitory and hid them in the storeroom of the ward next door. When a Doctor or Matron phoned to say a new admission was due we explained that the workmen had already been and removed the bed. Most times they found a spare bed in another ward. When the workmen did eventually arrive we told them that the bed was awaiting their collection. For as long as we could get away with this subterfuge our life - and the patients' - was that little easier and the ward less crowded.

About a third of our patients were nicknamed 'the softies' because their advanced age and dementia had long since replaced the violence of their younger years. Now they were harmless and caused very little trouble. Often they would spend all day walking up and down the day room talking to themselves or repeating the same thing over and over again. One, called Minnie, would not speak at all and would sit hunched up in a corner ignoring everyone. This would go on for weeks until she suddenly had an outburst of shouting and swearing. On these occasions she would often lash out at any patient or member of staff who happened to get in her way. The shouting and abuse would last for hours until she suddenly retreated back again into her silent world.

Another patient would raise her hand high above her and then lower it slowly. She would repeat this exercise hundreds of times during the day. We were so used to it that no one took any notice of it, but it went down like a lead balloon when we took her to the hospital cinema.

Another reason for the so called 'softies' name was their diets. Dentures, always in danger of being swallowed, often had to be removed and this, along with their advanced years, meant they were given an easily digested diet. Mince meat, mashed potato, milk puddings, jelly and custard or even sandwiches with the crusts removed.

I grew very fond of these harmless old ladies and became very protective towards them. Other patients on the ward had severe psychotic disorders and a large proportion also had epilepsy. This plus the side effects of the powerful drugs meant they were often violent and argumentative. Most of them were put to work in the laundry or the kitchen. It was a sight to behold each morning as they stomped off, each carrying a very large bag into which they stuffed all their worldly possessions. They constantly stole from each other and trusted no one, including the staff - the only solution, in their eyes, was to carry everything with them wherever they went. As they walked along muttering to each other they threatened dire consequences to any of the staff who dared to cross them.

I remember Grace vividly. She was very large, around fifteen stone. Being in her early forties she was also very strong. Over the years she had gained quite a reputation for being violent and aggressive. She wore her straight black hair tied back with a grubby ribbon and wore no make up except for a bright red lipstick which she daubed liberally over her lips. Her ensemble was completed by a long floral dress which billowed over her ample figure and sturdy legs. On her feet she wore thick ankle socks and heavy black shoes buckled on the side. In mixed company Grace would make a beeline for the nearest male. Quite what they thought when Grace rushed up to them I had no idea, that is, until my husband described his encounter with her. I can only say that Grace was in the right place where she was. She would have had one hell of an impact on the general public, and she was a typical bully. She could be awkward with any new member of staff, especially if they were young and inexperienced.

Patients who were old and frail would also suffer verbal or physical abuse but occasionally she would pick on a contemporary who was just as violent and she did not always come away unscathed. One morning she attacked an old lady in her eighties and we put her in a side room and locked the door both as a punishment and to protect the old lady. A furious Grace shouted to one of her cronies about how terribly she was being treated. Her friend promptly phoned Grace's sister and told her a tale of woe. A few minutes later I received a telephone call from her sister complaining bitterly about our treatment and demanding that we let her out of the side room. I explained why she was under lock and key, and I also reminded her that Grace was not held under section and was here on a voluntary basis. As she was so displeased with Grace's treatment perhaps she would like to come and collect her at a convenient time. There was a long silence from the other end of the phone line until she spoke again in a more conciliatory tone. She agreed that Grace could be very awkward, even difficult at times. She felt we were doing an excellent job of looking after her and that she was definitely in the best place. Reluctantly I agreed that she was probably right.

When the patients who went off to work left the ward we settled down to a period of peace and serenity. As the remaining patients were washed and fed Sister Alcock would prepare a breakfast special for the nurses. She made wonderful oatcakes which she fried with eggs, bacon, tomato, sausage and anything else that came to hand. After a busy morning it all tasted wonderful. On a Saturday it was even better. Saturday was always a quiet day and in the afternoon a nurse with four or five selected patients was dispatched to Leek. This was their weekly treat. They could wander around the town or do a little shopping in the market. It also gave the nurse a break from the ward.

My friend Jenny had been assigned to accompany the patients one Saturday and she could not wait to leave the ward and escape with her charges. By now you will have gathered that our patients could be a little unpredictable. It started on the bus with the patients shouting to each other and making rude comments to other passengers, and got progressively worse as the bus completed the short journey that seemed like a lifetime to my friend. The mayhem caused in the town reached a peak when one of the patients got lost and a frazzled Jenny prayed for the ground to open up beneath her.

The only bright spot in the whole afternoon as far as she was concerned came with the purchase of a large cream cake from Tiko's, the best cake shop in Leek. The cake was absolutely perfect. The prospect of a long bath, a bottle of wine and a slice of cream cake would make the memory of an horrendous afternoon fade. When a distraught Jenny finally brought her patients back to the ward the cream cake was put safely on one side. But Sister Alcock had gone to a great deal of trouble to provide us all with a nice tea, and the cream cake, she thought, would add the finishing touch. Jenny did not. The more comments Sister made about sharing the cake the more stubborn Jenny became. "Over my dead body" or "You must be joking" were milder replies. Eventually, half way through our tea, sensing the cake was in danger, Jenny got up to move the precious commodity. The next minute it fell from her hands and landed on the floor. Sister, usually so ponderous, moved like lightening and before anyone realised what was happening she scooped the now cracked cake onto a plate and cut it into several pieces. The look on Jenny's face had to be seen to be believed. I can still see it now. Tears were running down our faces with laughing so much. Even Jenny was laughing. Sister Alcock looked at everyone "Waste not want not" she said and handed each of us a piece.

If Jenny's trip to Leek was traumatic the ward outing was even worse. Time and finance permitting, and when staff availability would allow us, we endeavoured to take suitable patients on a summer outing. The young, uninitiated nurses saw these events as being pleasurable and quickly volunteered their services. Their perception of the outing was having a fun day at the seaside, ball games on the beach and maybe dipping a toe in the water - the sun no doubt beating down from a cloudless sky. Or alternatively a leisurely day in the countryside strolling by the river which meandered by a local hostelry where they could all have lunch - alfresco of course. Very enjoyable for staff and patients alike. After actually experiencing a few of these outings and discovering that reality did not match expectation they soon became reluctant to volunteer again.

The visit to Chester Zoo was planned for the second Tuesday in July. Our first priority was to decide which patients would be suitable for the excursion. The obvious candidates were the able bodied who were employed in various departments around the hospital plus the ones who helped on the wards. Several who were bed ridden or just unable to cope with the outside world had to be excluded immediately, as would the frail and some schizophenics. For the favoured, the outing became the main topic of conversation along with their usual bickering and moaning.

We had one particular patient who did not fit into any category. This lady's case notes showed her to be in her early forties. She had been privately educated and had a degree in English Literature. She had been employed as the personal assistant to the financial director of a large ceramics company. Having held the position for ten years she began to have trouble with her memory. It started in a small way when she simply forgot her handbag, except when it was returned she could not remember bringing it to the office in the first place. Her memory deteriorated more and more over a period of months until her employers reluctantly dispensed with her services. Within two years she was diagnosed as suffering from pre-senile dementia and admitted to St. Edwards. On good days she could dress and feed herself and have periods of lucidity when her memory returned. For the most part however her memory was non-existent. She would suddenly discard all her clothes for no apparent reason or empty her drawers and wardrobe onto the floor. She would leave taps running without recollection of what she had done. Later she would look totally bemused when she saw the results of her actions. Her husband who visited her on a regular basis often went away very upset after witnessing her unpredictable behaviour, but I think his main reason for being upset was because she did not recognise him. Even greater was the tragedy that, because she was only in her forties, the upsets and regrets would continue for many years.

Despite her problems she was a welcome addition to our outing and as the great day drew nigh the excitement in the ward increased. Came the day the ward was a hive of activity. It was vital that everyone was ready on time. Faces were washed, hair brushed, slides and ribbons in place. Shoes shone and dresses were pressed with treasured pieces of jewelry attached to give the final touch. By breakfast time they were far too excited to eat and they managed only a quick snack and a cup of tea before everyone was milling around the door and anxious to leave, It was just approaching eight o'clock and the coach was not due to arrive until nine! The next hour was filled by frequent visits to the toilet, squabbling over pocket money and debates about where they intended to sit on the coach.

Finally the coach arrived and a mass of patients, wheelchairs, walking sticks, umbrellas, spare cloths and tissues were all taken on board. One last check and I joined the patients along with a second nurse called Beryl, and Katie, our young student. Chester here we come. We eventually arrived at the zoo car park, looking outwardly quite a normal party as we began the unloading procedure. Chaos soon reigned as we tried to match excited patients with wheelchairs, simultaneously trying to supervise the mobile patients who were champing at the bit. The hour before lunch went reasonably well with the able bodied helping with the wheelchairs and good humour and banter kept everyone in good spirits.

We visited the children's Pets Corner hoping this would appeal to everyone. It certainly did and in doing so provided one of our treasured moments. As the patients stroked and fed the small animals, Katie pointed to Martha standing on her own. Martha was a long term patient who suffered from a psychotic illness. Despite the best efforts of doctors and nurses and changes in medication Martha had deteriorated markedly over the past few months. She would sit in the ward in silence, never speaking, devoid of any emotion and seemingly unaware of our presence. As we looked towards Martha, over by the goats, we thought we saw a flicker of a smile. It was almost like a miracle. Very slowly a big smile appeared and her face and eyes lit up. Tentatively she approached the goats and reached out to touch them. Goats however are goats and the sleeve of Martha's coat was too much of a temptation. As they began to chomp we had to intervene and the moment was gone. Even so we were delighted with this small but significant breakthrough.

Lunch-time arrived and we headed for the far end of the zoo where seats had been reserved in the restaurant. A waiter greeted us and kindly offered to do a head count for us. Something was not quite right - the patient number was correct but we were one nurse short. The problem was resolved when I pointed out that Beryl may be in 'mufti' but she would object strongly to being confused with the patients - we kept that little tit-bit to ourselves. It was only when we had got seated that we realised that if Beryl was a nurse we were still one body short. A quick check revealed that Mary R. was missing.

Mary had long been trusted to travel to Leek by herself on occasions and was more than capable of looking after herself so we decided to proceed with lunch. Afterwards as the main party went off to look at the larger animals I set off in the opposite direction. One way or another Mary had to be found. As I approached the entrance I spotted her on the other side of the railing sitting on a bench looking most forlorn. When she saw me she rushed up to the railings, raised her fist and swore at me. Her feelings flowed in a torrent of colourful language as she told me how she had gone to a kiosk for cigarettes only to return to find we had all gone into the zoo. As we had a group ticket she was unable to follow. The only way she could gain entry was to use her own money but this would have been totally against the grain. Instead she sat and fumed for several hours. To Mary this was quite logical and now I had to placate her. Free entry and a fish and chip dinner did the trick and after my insincere apologies we set off in search of the others. By retracing out steps we found the rest of the party.

Katie and Beryl were discussing the reactions of the public. Some comments had been very derogatory even to the extent of saying that the mentally handicapped should not be allowed to mix with normal people. In direct contrast several people stopped to say hello and ask if we needed assistance with the wheelchairs or negotiating the steps. We only hoped that society would develop more tolerance as it came into increasing contact with the less fortunate.

The rest of the afternoon passed peacefully enough as we wandered around the zoo. The monkeys especially kept the patients amused! It was with reluctance that they finally left the area and headed for the gift shop to spend the last of their money before returning to the coach. We arrived back at St. Edward's that evening totally worn out. Except for possibly an odd case of sickness or diarrhoea from overeating, the patients were unlikely to cause the night shift any problems at all that night.

Beryl decided she would seriously consider the merits of early retirement and Katie said she felt more like ninety than nineteen. We had aching heads and feet, but despite everything we had enjoyed it. But! - we were definitely not volunteering for next year's outing!

Nursing the mentally ill did have its drawbacks but it had so many more advantages. The friendship on the wards, those special nurses, the laughter and despair with the patients. Most of all it gave me a sense of achievement and satisfaction.

Reflections

As I was writing this story I could not help thinking how ordinary my life was, and how lucky I was to have led such an ordinary existence. I think we all have our dreams and aspirations. Some are achieved and others fall by the wayside. But our formative years remain dear regardless of the era. In my case it is the freedom of my childhood that remains dear. Freedom to wander for miles and miles in complete safety. The boundaries of our village stretched from Combes Valley to Shaffalong, from Folly Lane to Leekbrook and we roamed every inch either on secondhand bicycles or on foot. Traffic was light enough to be of no concern even to the extent of allowing us to play games in the road without too much fear of interruption.

Not only were we innocent we were totally naive. Television, with its graphic exposure, was years away and we were happy enough to simply enjoy a life that had changed little over the years. The problems come in later years when we make comparisons or resent change, but on considered reflection we see only too well the need for progress.

Older readers will remember vividly the closet at the top of the garden, but do they remember the 'muck men' who came along each week to empty the containers. We remember long hot summers when we roamed the fields or played cricket until ten at night, but meteorological records prove that our summers were no better or no worse than any others and it is not until the 1990s that temperatures become significantly higher.

The main difference between then and now is freedom of children. I am sure today's children still roam the countryside but not to the same degree. A child takes its life in its hands by simply crossing a road and the stories of crime, abduction and assault that bombard our television screens are enough to fill any young mother with apprehension. Little wonder we feel safer when children are within shouting distance.

Ironically it is television and now the computer that have brought about the greatest change. Electricity did not reach some parts of the village until after the War and the introduction of TV was seen as a great innovation. And so it should. Not only did it remove much of our ignorance and naivety, it illustrated at the touch of a button events that were occurring all over the world, in places we could never have dreamt of seeing.

The battle for our minds, and in some cases our souls, was fought out by the B.B.C. and the independent television stations. The result was a foregone conclusion, with money from advertising influencing the programmes and the hyperbole influencing the viewers. To the youngster who liked sport the introduction of satellite TV and BSkyB must seem heaven sent. But, when they are watching, they are not playing.

Television has become a great disappointment. We all watch it of course but my heart sinks when I think what might have been. Now we face a multitude of channels all fighting to attract viewers with an ever increasing amount of trivia and an ever reducing amount of quality. Yet electricity has transformed life. Second to our freedom comes the convenience of modern life. Here my generation was in the dark ages. I can think of nothing to recommend life without electricity, the motor car, running water, toilets and central heating. On that score today's children win hands down. They are also better dressed, better fed and healthier.

In terms of education I have mixed feelings. Today's youngsters seem bright, confident and responsive. They cope well enough with the latest technology. My grandchildren operate the video recorder and computer without a second thought and their level of conversation leaves me feeling confident in the future. Even so I feel like an outcast in lamenting the passing of elitism. I know I would never have been one of the academic elite but I cannot help feeling that in our quest for equality it is the elite who have suffered and not the failures who have gained. Pursuit of the lowest common denominator is doomed to failure and I feel certain that as university degrees become commonplace their value will be undermined.

But changes are inevitable. I am biased of course but, although I have concerns about modern childhood, I confess to rather liking today's youngsters. I like their confidence and, given the chance, they display ample courtesy and consideration. We ought to be quite proud of our offspring and the life they lead.

Some aspects of my childhood are unlikely to return. The slow pace of life with canal barges and local railways dominating the scene is also a thing of the past. I am so pleased it was a part of my childhood. Many of the wild flowers and birds have gone forever. It is this that saddens me most. How long is it since you saw Ragged Robin growing in the hedgerows and what has happened to the Lady Smock? I occasionally come across a clump of Lady Smock in a corner of a damp field where pesticide has failed to penetrate, but I cannot remember when I last saw a local field awash with those mauve flowers.

As for the birds, even the common House Sparrow seems in decline and when you look for Skylarks, Curlew and Peewits the decline is even more noticeable. I am sure they still exist, albeit in smaller numbers, but the occasional encounter does not begin to compensate for the flocks of Peewits that colonised the fields around Basford or the Curlews that circled over the moors around Ringe Hay. Once again I think my childhood had the advantage.

In reality we should hang our heads in shame. It is not the fault of the youngsters that flowers and birds are in decline. It is our generation that allowed it to happen. How we could have prevented it I do not know. We can hardly blame the farmer for being efficient and at the moment they are struggling hard enough to make a living anyway. There seems to be a huge contradiction in our lives. The western world produces vast quantities of food. America is said to throw away as much food as it produces. Yet other parts of the world are starving.

In our pursuit of profit and easy living we have changed the countryside for the worse. Perhaps we can say that what today's children have never had they will not miss. For my part I think we have passed on a blighted inheritance.

But I would hate to end on a dismal note so I will remind you that all is not lost. We recently visited a wild flower nursery near Nottingham. I cannot begin to describe what memories were evoked as we walked through the fields. The fragrances and the colours took me back to my childhood. The nursery is a thriving concern and sells plants and seeds nationwide. Obviously people still care. And in Southern Ireland Vera and I came across a small village where a group of elderly people were having a break from their toils in the church yard. The ground all around them was awash with colour. What they had done was simple in the extreme although quite hard work initially. All the ground had been cleared of weeds, thistles and coarse grass and a layer of a wild flower compost had been spread everywhere. The result was spectacular and far, far better than anything man could have produced. As a bonus the insects and the birds were also back and no doubt spreading seed and pollen here, there and everywhere. Now that would be a legacy to hand down!

A Cheddleton Bowls Team.

Cheddleton Band 1920s

Cheddleton 1948

T. Alcock, J. Pearson, J. Thomas, P. Shenton, ? , T. Harrison

D. Pearson, ? Mason, E. Pearson, A. Pearson, F. Rutter, S. Alcock, G. Bunker, L. Pearson

J. Wheeldon, J. Pearson, ? , ? , J. Rane, ? , J. Cooper, G. Kirkham, Mrs Cooper

G. Tait, ? , J.T. Hedley, W. Dishley, R. Goldstraw, H. Barber, ? , T. Padin, H. Leedham, J. Shenton.

Cheddleton Band 1960s.

Mrs M. Pegg

Geoffrey Fisher

A Berresford's bus by
the Coffee Tavern
and the cattle market
in Leek.

Harry Bold outside
his shop in the canal
basin (later to be the
Flintlock restaurant).

The Canal Basin early 20th century.

Cheddleton Station Easter 1960